PRACTICAL
MDX QUERIES

for Microsoft® SQL Server®
Analysis Services 2008

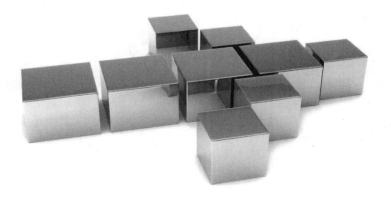

About the Author

Art Tennick (Brighton, UK) has worked in relational database design and SQL queries for over 20 years. He has been involved in multidimensional database design, cubes, data mining, DMX, and MDX queries for 10 years. Based in the UK, he has been a software consultant, trainer, and writer for some 25 years. Recently, he has worked with several major retail and banking corporations to implement BI solutions using Microsoft SQL Server, SSAS, SSIS, SSRS, and Excel 2007/2010. This is his 17th book and he has also written over 300 articles for computer magazines in the USA, the UK, and Ireland. His Web site is www.MrCube.net.

About the Technical Editor

Deepak Puri is a Business Intelligence Consultant and has been working with SQL Server Analysis Services since 2000. Deepak is currently a Microsoft SQL Server MVP with a focus on OLAP. His interest in OLAP technology arose from working with large volumes of call center telecom data at a large insurance company. In addition, Deepak has also worked with performance data and key performance indicators (KPIs) for new business processes.

Deepak has participated in the technical editing of three books on Analysis Services and the MDX language. He currently resides in Northeastern Ohio.

PRACTICAL MDX QUERIES

for Microsoft® SQL Server® Analysis Services 2008

Art Tennick

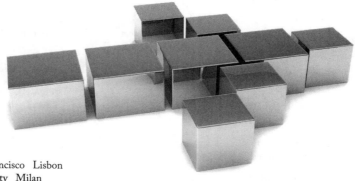

New York   Chicago   San Francisco   Lisbon
London   Madrid   Mexico City   Milan
New Delhi   San Juan   Seoul   Singapore
Sydney   Toronto

The McGraw·Hill Companies

Library of Congress Cataloging-in-Publication Data

Tennick, Art.
     Practical MDX queries for Microsoft® for SQL server® analysis services
2008 / Art Tennick.
          p.   cm.
     Includes index.
     ISBN 978-0-07-171336-8 (alk. paper)
     1. Business intelligence.   2. MDX (Computer program language)   I. Title.
HD38.7.T46   2010
005.13'3—dc22   2010015778

McGraw-Hill books are available at special quantity discounts to use as premiums and sales promotions, or for use in corporate training programs. To contact a representative, please e-mail us at bulksales@mcgraw-hill.com.

Practical MDX Queries for Microsoft® SQL Server® Analysis Services 2008

1234567890   DOC DOC   109876543210

ISBN   978-0-07-171336-8
MHID   0-07-171336-0

Sponsoring Editor Wendy Rinaldi	**Indexer** Karin Arrigoni
Editorial Supervisor Patty Mon	**Production Supervisor** George Anderson
Project Manager Madhu Bhardwaj, Glyph International	**Composition** Glyph International
Acquisitions Coordinator Joya Anthony	**Illustration** Glyph International
Technical Editor Deepak Puri	**Art Director, Cover** Jeff Weeks
Copy Editor Bart Reed	**Cover Designer** Jeff Weeks
Proofreader Laura Bowman	

For Kang Hong Ying, lovely Liaoning lady.

Contents at a Glance

Contents

Acknowledgments

Thank you to my editor, Wendy Rinaldi. In particular, she demonstrated remarkable vision, enthusiasm, and patience. Also thanks to Joya Anthony for her efforts in getting my original draft into a publishable book and to Melinda Lytle who helped with the graphics. Finally, I am indebted to Deepak Puri who displayed remarkable insight as the technical reviewer of the MDX queries.

Introduction

MDX

Business intelligence (BI) is a very rapidly growing area of the software market. Microsoft's core product in this field is SQL Server Analysis Services (SSAS). It is revolutionizing how companies view and work with data. Its purpose is to turn data into information, giving meaning to the data. There are two main objects in SSAS that support this goal—cubes and data-mining models. If these can be visualized easily, the information they contain is transformed into intelligence, thus leading to timely and effective decision making. Cube information can be extracted and visualized with Multidimensional Expressions (MDX) queries. Data-mining model information can be extracted and visualized with Data Mining Extensions (DMX) queries. This book is devoted to cubes and the MDX language. It takes you from first principles in MDX query writing and builds into more and more sophisticated queries. This book is a practical one—with lots of syntax to try on nearly every page (and you can copy and paste from the download files for this book, if you prefer not to type).

Prerequisites

You will need two databases. First, the SSAS Adventure Works DW 2008 database (called Adventure Works DW in SSAS 2005), which contains the Adventure Works cube. The MDX queries are written against this cube. Second, the SQL Server AdventureWorksDW2008 database (called AdventureWorksDW in SQL Server 2005), which provides the source data required by the SSAS Adventure Works DW 2008 database.

Installing Adventure Works

You can download the required SSAS database (with the Adventure Works cube) and SQL Server database from www.codeplex.com (both 2008 and 2005 versions). As of this writing, the URL was http://www.codeplex.com/MSFTDBProdSamples/Release/ ProjectReleases.aspx?ReleaseID=16040. Choose SQL Server 2008 or SQL Server 2005 from the Releases box. URLs can change—if you have difficulty then search www.codeplex.com on Adventure Works Samples.

SSAS 2008

Before you begin the download, you might want to check the two hyperlinks, Database Prerequisites and Installing Databases. Download and run SQL2008.AdventureWorks All Databases.x86.msi (there are also 64-bit versions, x64 and ia64). As the installation proceeds, you will have to choose an instance name for your SQL Server. When the installation finishes, you will have some new SQL Server databases, including AdventureWorksDW2008 (used to build the SSAS Adventure Works cube). You will not have the cube just yet.

SSAS 2005

The download file is called AdventureWorksBICI.msi (there are also 64-bit versions, x64 and IA64). With 2005, you can also go through Setup or Control Panel to add the samples—this is not possible in 2008. Unlike in 2008, the download and subsequent installation do not result in the new SQL Server source database appearing under SQL Server in SSMS. You have to manually attach the database. You can do this from SSMS (right-click the Databases folder and choose Attach) if you have some DBA knowledge. Or you might ask your SQL Server DBA to do this for you. If you click the Release Notes hyperlink on the download page, you will find out how to do this from SQL—but this is an MDX book! You will not have the cube just yet.

Creating the Adventure Works Cube

This cube is used by all the MDX queries in this book. Here's how to deploy it:

1. Navigate to C:\Program Files\Microsoft SQL Server\100\Tools\Samples\ AdventureWorks 2008 Analysis Services\Project (C:\Program Files\Microsoft SQL Server\90\Tools\Samples\AdventureWorks Analysis Services\Project for 2005).
2. Depending on your edition of SSAS, open the Enterprise or Standard folder.
3. Double-click the Adventure Works.sln file. This will open BIDS.
4. In Solution Explorer, right-click the Adventure Works project, which is probably in bold. If you can't see Solution Explorer, click View | Solution Explorer. The project will be called Adventure Works DW 2008 (for SSAS 2008 Enterprise Edition) or Adventure Works DW 2008 SE (for SSAS 2008 Standard Edition) or Adventure Works DW (for SSAS 2005 Enterprise Edition) or Adventure Works DW Standard Edition (for SSAS 2005 Standard Edition).
5. Click Deploy (then click Yes if prompted). After a few minutes, you should see Deploy Succeeded message on the status bar and Deployment Completed Successfully in the Deployment Progress window.

If the deployment fails, try these steps:

1. Right-click the project and choose Properties. Go to the Deployment page and check that the Server entry points to your SSAS (*not* SQL Server) instance—you might have a named SSAS instance rather than a default instance, or your SSAS may be on a remote server.
2. Right-click Adventure Works.ds (under the Data Sources folder in Solution Explorer) and choose Open. Click Edit and check that the Server name entry points to your SQL Server (*not* SSAS) instance—you might have a named SQL Server instance rather than a default instance, or your SQL Server may be on a remote server.
3. Try and deploy again.

Source Code

All the source code for the queries in this book is available for download. You can simply copy and paste into the query editor to save you typing. You can copy and paste individual queries or copy and paste blocks of code. If you do the latter, make sure you highlight only the relevant code before you run the query.

You can download the source code from www.mhprofessional.com/computingdownload.

Acronyms

- ▶ **BI**   Business intelligence
- ▶ **BIDS**   SQL Server Business Intelligence Development Studio
- ▶ **DMX**   Data Mining Extensions
- ▶ **KPI**   Key performance indicator
- ▶ **MDX**   MultiDimensional Expressions
- ▶ **SQL**   Structured Query Language
- ▶ **SSAS**   SQL Server Analysis Services
- ▶ **SSIS**   SQL Server Integration Services
- ▶ **SSMS**   SQL Server Management Studio
- ▶ **SSRS**   SQL Server Reporting Services
- ▶ **XMLA**   XML for Analysis

SSAS 2008 or SSAS 2005?

The MDX queries in this book are primarily for SSAS 2008. Fortunately, over 99 percent also work against SSAS 2005. One minor exception is the Create KPI syntax (one query in the book), which was introduced in SSAS 2008. Also, the dates in the SSAS 2008 and SSAS 2005 sample cubes are slightly different. In SSAS 2005, you will not see the calendar year CY 2006 nor will you see the fiscal year FY 2007. As a result, there may be a few small differences in the results of just some of your queries that return dates.

Enterprise/Developer Edition or Standard Edition?

It makes little difference which edition you use. All the queries work against the Enterprise/Developer Edition of SSAS. Over 99 percent will also work against the Standard Edition. SSAS Standard Edition does not support Select statements against perspectives (one query in the book).

Writing Queries

To write a query, follow these steps:

1. Open SSMS.
2. If prompted to connect, click Cancel.
3. Click File | New | Analysis Services MDX Query.
4. Click Connect in the dialog box.

5. From the drop-down on the toolbar, choose the Adventure Works DW 2008 database.

6. Make sure the Adventure Works cube is selected in the Cube drop-down just to the left of the query editor window. The cube metadata should be visible in the Metadata pane.

7. Type, or type and drag, or copy and paste to create the query.

8. Click the Execute button on the toolbar.

There are many other ways of opening the query editor. Here's a popular alternative:

1. In Object Explorer, right-click the SSAS database Adventure Works DW 2008 (Adventure Works DW in SSAS 2005).

2. Click New Query | MDX.

3. Make sure the Adventure Works cube is selected in the Cube drop-down just to the left of the query editor window. The cube metadata should be visible in the Metadata pane.

Chapter Content

The MDX you learn can be used in many places. These include SQL Server Reporting Services (SSRS), SQL Server Integration Services (SSIS), Performance Point Server, and your own .NET Windows forms and web pages. In addition, you can extend your SQL and DMX queries by embedding MDX code. By and large, all the MDX in the book is divided into chapters based on functionality. The chapters are as follows.

Chapter 1: Hello World: Easy Yet Effective Queries

This is a short chapter to get you started. It has a few queries so you get a flavor of the power and elegance of the MDX language.

Chapter 2: Astrophysical: Playing with Dimensions

This chapter shows you how to work with dimensions, hierarchies, levels, and members. It's quite possibly the most difficult chapter in the whole book—especially if you are not familiar yet with the concepts of dimensions and hierarchies. Understanding them is vital if you want to write meaningful and powerful MDX.

Chapter 3: Families and Friends: Navigating Dimensions

Here we explore moving up, down, and across dimensions and hierarchies. The general term for doing this is navigation. MDX allows you to navigate both horizontally and vertically. MDX (unlike SQL) is positionally aware—it knows where you are in the cube and can help you in your navigation.

Chapter 4: Bringing Order: Sorting Results

This chapter introduces various ways of sorting the results of your queries. Business intelligence reports often have a requirement to put the information in some kind of order—whether numeric or alphabetic. This chapter shows you how to do this.

Chapter 5: Slice, Dice, and Filter: Using Where and Filter

Often, you will want only a subset of your dimension members and measure values. This can be achieved by slicing and dicing with a Where clause. An alternative approach involves using criteria with a Filter function. The MDX clause is not the same as an SQL one—hopefully, by the end of t[...] be proficient at using it in MDX.

Chapter 6: Using the Abacus: Introduction to Calculations

In general, the measures in your cube are based directly or indirectly on the columns in your fact table in your star schema. However, it's likely your reports will need further metrics. These are often based on the existing measures in some way. One way to devise these new measures is to use MDX query calculations. Here we explore how to do this. In addition, we take a look at creating non-measure members and creating our own sets of data.

Chapter 7: Is Time a Dimension? Working with Dates and Times

Nearly every cube in the world has a date or time dimension. MDX provides many rich features that help you to analyze your data across history. In this chapter, you are introduced to lots of functions for manipulating dates and times. These will help you produce brilliant business intelligence reports!

Chapter 8: Clockwork: Calculations Using Dates and Times

The previous chapter introduces the MDX to extract and manipulate dates. This chapter combines the MDX you learn there with aggregate and other functions. Here you get to use these aggregate and other functions to produce totals, subtotals, and changes across time. This is a big part of business intelligence reporting.

Chapter 9: Venn Diagrams: Visualizing and Manipulating Sets

Here's a wide-ranging chapter on working with sets and members of sets. By the end of the chapter, you'll be able to create, visualize, and manipulate sets.

Chapter 10: Views on Cubes: Working with Subcubes

If you are familiar with SQL, you may use views. One use of a view on a relational table is to present only a part of the table. Often, you will want to work on only a part of a cube. The SSAS versions of SQL views are called perspectives, subselects, and subcubes. Here we get to exploit those perspectives, subselects, and subcubes.

Chapter 11: Not All There: Dealing with Empty Cells

Cubes are often pretty big. They contain lots and lots of data. However, there will also be many gaps. For example, it's unlikely that every customer bought every product on every single day. There will be missing or null data. Sometimes, you want to see null values—maybe zero sales are of interest. Sometimes, the null values are a distraction and you will want to hide them. This chapter concentrates on displaying and hiding empty cells.

Chapter 12: Smiley Faces: Working with Key Performance Indicators (KPIs)

Key performance indicators (KPIs) are a vital part of business intelligence. At a glance, you can see how well you are doing without having to dig down and analyze individual metrics. They are a high-level overview of results—and of results against targets. Here we explore using, modifying, formatting, and creating KPIs in MDX.

Chapter 13: Hodgepodge: A Chapter of Miscellaneous Techniques

This is a catchall chapter for topics that do not fit easily into earlier chapters. Formatting and conditional formatting are investigated. There are a1 drill through and drill down on the cube.

Chapter 14: After You Finish

Throughout this book, you'll be using SSMS to write your MDX queries and display the results. It's unlikely that your users will have SSMS—indeed, it's not recommended for end users because SSMS is simply too powerful and potentially dangerous. This chapter presents some alternative software and methods for getting MDX query results to the end user.

Chapter 1

Hello World: Easy Yet Effective Queries

Welcome to MDX. This short chapter is designed to get you started. It has a few queries so you get a taste of the power and elegance of the MDX language. It's not important at this stage that you understand the syntax of the sample queries—all will become clear as you progress through the examples in the rest of the book. Also, don't be misled by any initial and superficial similarity to SQL—MDX is a completely different language from SQL!

▶ **Key concepts**   Cube, columns, rows, cells, dimensions, measures, default measure

▶ **Keywords**   Select, From, Where, Columns, Rows, Non Empty

Hello World MDX Query 1/4

Type in the following query in the MDX editor in SSMS (SQL Server Management Studio), and make sure you have a connection to the Adventure Works database (it should be showing in the drop-down on your toolbar). Or, if you have downloaded the files that accompany the book, you can copy and paste. You can also combine typing with dragging and dropping. In the Metadata pane, you can drag in the name of the cube, [Adventure Works]. If you do so, make sure you remove the highlight—SSAS (SQL Server Analysis Services) tries to execute the highlight in isolation from the rest of the code. Alternatively, you can highlight the full query. Click the Execute button on the toolbar to run the query (or press F5 or CTRL-E or ALT-X, or select Query | Execute from the menu bar). Lots of ways to run your MDX queries!

Syntax

```
-- hello world 1/4
-- this is a comment like the line before it
select
from
[Adventure Works]
```

Result

$80,450,596.98

Analysis

Well done. MDX is not that difficult. The result you should see underneath your query is $80,450,596.98. Not that it means that much, just yet. It's the super grand total from the cube—that is, for all products and all dates and all resellers and all locations and so on. In fact, it's the super grand total for Reseller Sales Amount—not that you can tell by looking at either the syntax or the result. Reseller Sales Amount is something called the default measure of the cube—it's the measure (or fact, metric, or figure) that appears unless you specify otherwise. There is much more on this in the next and subsequent chapters.

Hello World MDX Query 2/4

This is our second query. It has an identical result to our first query. Note the addition of the Where clause.

Syntax

```
-- hello world 2/4
select
from
[Adventure Works]
where [Measures].[Reseller Sales Amount]
```

Result

```
$80,450,596.98
```

Analysis

Yes, this is the same answer. Here we have explicitly requested the Reseller Sales Amount measure. One way of doing so is to include it in the Where clause. In MDX, a Where clause is called a *slicer*. Because Reseller Sales Amount is the default measure, the Where clause is not necessary, but it does make the MDX more explicit. Maybe it would be nice to see this labeled as Reseller Sales Amount in the output (which we'll do in the query after the next one).

Hello World MDX Query 3/4

Here the Where clause has changed. This time the slicer is asking for Internet Sales Amount.

Syntax

```
-- hello world 3/4
select
from
[Adventure Works]
where [Measures].[Internet Sales Amount]
```

Result

$29,358,677.22

Analysis

When you reference measures, you must precede the measure name with either Measures or [Measures]. The use of square brackets is optional but is considered good practice because it shows your metadata clearly. Note that Internet Sales Amount is entered as [Internet Sales Amount]. The square brackets here are obligatory because of the spaces in the name. Your answer is now $29,358,677.22—the super grand total for Internet (not reseller) sales for all products and all dates and all customers and so on.

Hello World MDX Query 4/4

No Where clause this time. Instead, the Reseller Sales Amount is requested on the columns.

Syntax

```
-- hello world 4/4
select
[Measures].[Reseller Sales Amount]
on columns
from
[Adventure Works]
```

Result

Reseller Sales Amount

$80,450,596.98

Analysis

This probably looks a little better. Now it's obvious that the measure in the result is indeed for reseller sales and not for Internet sales or for any other measure. The important syntax change is the column specification that dictates what appears across the Columns axis of the result—an MDX result is often called a *cellset*.

Dimension Data on Columns

The previous query placed a measure across the columns. By contrast, our query this time places dimension data from the Date dimension along the columns. Strictly speaking, I should say non-measure dimension data. As you will see later, [Measures] can be considered a dimension as well. This is a little confusing if you are new to MDX and you have a relational star schema where the dimension tables (which don't contain facts) are distinct from the fact table (which does contain the facts or the measures). A dimension is anything that can go on an axis. The last query placed Reseller Sales Amount on an axis, thus [Measures] qualifies as a dimension too.

Syntax

```
-- adding dimension data to columns
select
[Date].[Calendar].[Calendar Year]
on columns
from
[Adventure Works]
```

Result

CY 2001	CY 2002	CY 2003	CY 2004	CY 2006
$8,065,435.31	$24,144,429.65	$32,202,669.43	$16,038,062.60	(null)

Analysis

[Date].[Calendar].[Calendar Year] is in the format [Dimension].[Hierarchy].[Level]. We are asking for all of the calendar years. Notice that CY 2005 is missing. This means that CY 2005 simply does not exist within the dimension. The cells have values for the default measure Reseller Sales Amount.

More Than One

There is now a comma-separated list for the column specification. The braces around the two entries are obligatory—the query will fail without them. The next chapter (over the course of a couple queries) shows just what they do.

Syntax

```
-- and a total column
select
{[Date].[Calendar].[Calendar Year],[Date].[Calendar]}
on columns
from
[Adventure Works]
```

Result

CY 2001	CY 2002	CY 2003	CY 2004	CY 2006	All Periods
$8,065,435.31	$24,144,429.65	$32,202,669.43	$16,038,062.60	(null)	$80,450,596.98

Analysis

[Date].[Calendar] is in the form [Dimension].[Hierarchy]. It's the very top of the hierarchy and is called All Periods. It's the total (or aggregation) of the individual calendar years: $80,450,596.98, which we met earlier. The other figures (cells) add up to this total.

Dimension Data on Rows

Let's exploit the second axis in our two-dimensional display. It's the Rows axis. Be aware that a comma (,) separates the column specification from the row specification.

Syntax

```
-- adding dimension data to rows
select
{ [Date].[Calendar].[Calendar Year],[Date].[Calendar] }
on columns,
[Product].[Product Categories].[Category]
on rows
from
[Adventure Works]
```

Result

	CY 2001	CY 2002	CY 2003	CY 2004	CY 2006	All Periods
Accessories	$20,235.36	$92,735.35	$296,532.88	$161,794.33	(null)	$571,297.93
Bikes	$7,395,348.63	$19,956,014.67	$25,551,775.07	$13,399,243.18	(null)	$66,302,381.56
Clothing	$34,376.34	$485,587.15	$871,864.19	$386,013.16	(null)	$1,777,840.84
Components	$615,474.98	$3,610,092.47	$5,482,497.29	$2,091,011.92	(null)	$11,799,076.66

Analysis

Two dimensions on two axes. I imagine your cube (like Adventure Works) has rather more than two dimensions. But we are limited to a two-axis display! Fortunately, two axes do not confine us to two dimensions (how good is your cosmology?). There is a very useful Crossjoin function in MDX that allows us to load (by nesting) more than one dimension on a single axis. Two axes (Columns and Rows) do not limit us to only two dimensions! There is much more on Crossjoin discussed later in the book.

A Total Row

Once again, the braces around the two entries for the rows specification are vital.

Syntax

```
-- and a total row
select
{[Date].[Calendar].[Calendar Year],[Date].[Calendar]}
on columns,
{[Product].[Product Categories].[Category],[Product].[Product Categories]}
on rows
from
[Adventure Works]
```

Result

	CY 2001	CY 2002	CY 2003	CY 2004	CY 2006	All Periods
Accessories	$20,235.36	$92,735.35	$296,532.88	$161,794.33	(null)	$571,297.93
Bikes	$7,395,348.63	$19,956,014.67	$25,551,775.07	$13,399,243.18	(null)	$66,302,381.56
Clothing	$34,376.34	$485,587.15	$871,864.19	$386,013.16	(null)	$1,777,840.84
Components	$615,474.98	$3,610,092.47	$5,482,497.29	$2,091,011.92	(null)	$11,799,076.66
All Products	$8,065,435.31	$24,144,429.65	$32,202,669.43	$16,038,062.60	(null)	$80,450,596.98

Analysis

This is quite a cool query for so early in your MDX career. Try doing that in SQL against a relational (normalized or even denormalized) database! You might recognize the cell, $80,450,596.98, in the bottom-right corner.

Hiding Nulls

You might want to hide CY 2006 because there are no reseller sales for that year. Here we have Non Empty before the column specification.

Syntax

```
-- hiding nulls
select
non empty {[Date].[Calendar].[Calendar Year],[Date].[Calendar]}
on columns,
{[Product].[Product Categories].[Category],[Product].[Product Categories]}
on rows
from
[Adventure Works]
```

Result

	CY 2001	CY 2002	CY 2003	CY 2004	All Periods
Accessories	$20,235.36	$92,735.35	$296,532.88	$161,794.33	$571,297.93
Bikes	$7,395,348.63	$19,956,014.67	$25,551,775.07	$13,399,243.18	$66,302,381.56
Clothing	$34,376.34	$485,587.15	$871,864.19	$386,013.16	$1,777,840.84
Components	$615,474.98	$3,610,092.47	$5,482,497.29	$2,091,011.92	$11,799,076.66
All Products	$8,065,435.31	$24,144,429.65	$32,202,669.43	$16,038,062.60	$80,450,596.98

Analysis

To show or hide null values is a business decision. The result might look better without CY 2006. Then again, it might be important to know that 2006 sales are null (or empty or zero). If you were to browse a cube as a pivot table in Excel 2007, BIDS, or SSMS, the empty cells are hidden by default—although there are options to display them. This is the opposite behavior to the MDX query editor, which shows empty cells by default.

Displaying a Different Measure

Here, a Where slicer is used to change to Internet Sales Amount from the default Reseller Sales Amount that was used implicitly in the last query.

Syntax

```
-- different measure
select
{ [Date].[Calendar].[Calendar Year],[Date].[Calendar] }
on columns,
{ [Product].[Product Categories].[Category],[Product].[Product Categories] }
on rows
from
[Adventure Works]
where [Measures].[Internet Sales Amount]
```

Result

	CY 2001	CY 2002	CY 2003	CY 2004	CY 2006	All Periods
Accessories	(null)	(null)	$293,709.71	$407,050.25	(null)	$700,759.96
Bikes	$3,266,373.66	$6,530,343.53	$9,359,102.62	$9,162,324.85	(null)	$28,318,144.65
Clothing	(null)	(null)	$138,247.97	$201,524.64	(null)	$339,772.61
Components	(null)	(null)	(null)	(null)	(null)	(null)
All Products	$3,266,373.66	$6,530,343.53	$9,791,060.30	$9,770,899.74	(null)	$29,358,677.22

Analysis

The column and row headings (captions) remain the same. However, the values in the cells have changed. The cell at the bottom-right corner is now about 29 million dollars and not about 80 million dollars.

Hiding Nulls Again

Here we have the last query in this introductory "Hello World" chapter. It tidies up the previous query by using Non Empty on both axes to hide null values.

Syntax

```
-- hiding nulls again
select
non empty { [Date].[Calendar].[Calendar Year],[Date].[Calendar] }
on columns,
non empty { [Product].[Product Categories].[Category],
[Product].[Product Categories] }
on rows
from
[Adventure Works]
where [Measures].[Internet Sales Amount]
```

Result

	CY 2001	CY 2002	CY 2003	CY 2004	All Periods
Accessories	(null)	(null)	$293,709.71	$407,050.25	$700,759.96
Bikes	$3,266,373.66	$6,530,343.53	$9,359,102.62	$9,162,324.85	$28,318,144.65
Clothing	(null)	(null)	$138,247.97	$201,524.64	$339,772.61
All Products	$3,266,373.66	$6,530,343.53	$9,791,060.30	$9,770,899.74	$29,358,677.22

Analysis

Non Empty is used twice—on the columns and on the rows. CY 2006 has gone as before. But Components has disappeared from the rows too. CY 2001 and Clothing both survive the use of Non Empty even though they have null values in some of their cells. Non Empty operates on the whole column (or row) and not on part of the column (or row). Thus CY 2001 is still there as there is a non-null value ($3,266,373.66) for the sales of Bikes in that year.

Chapter 2

Astrophysical: Playing with Dimensions

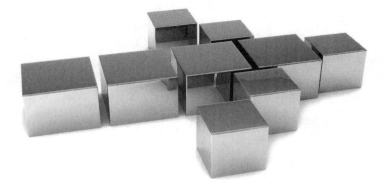

This chapter shows you how to work with dimensions, hierarchies, levels, and members. It's quite possibly the most difficult chapter in the whole book—especially if you are not familiar yet with the concepts of dimensions and hierarchies. Understanding them is vital if you want to write meaningful and powerful MDX.

▶ **Key concepts**   Multiple-hierarchy dimensions, attribute hierarchies, user hierarchies, displaying members

▶ **Keywords**   Select, Columns, Rows, .members, Crossjoin

Single-Hierarchy Dimension

The Sales Channel dimension contains just the one attribute, also called Sales Channel. Even though it is simply an attribute (probably a source column in a star schema relational database), it is also a hierarchy. By default, all attributes have an All level back in the dimension design in BIDS. Attribute hierarchies are represented as blue rectangles composed of six small squares in the Metadata pane of the query editor window. If a dimension should contain just the one attribute, it will not normally include any user-defined hierarchies, which usually require at least two attribute hierarchies to create two or more separate levels (in addition to the All level at the top). However, it is technically possible to create a user-defined hierarchy from a single attribute.

Syntax

```
-- single-hierarchy dimension
select
[Sales Channel] -- dimension
on columns
from
[Adventure Works]
```

Result

$80,450,596.98

Analysis

Here only the dimension is specified for the Columns axis. By default, it returns the default member of the attribute hierarchy. Usually, the default member is at the All level of the dimension's attribute hierarchy. The default member can be changed in BIDS. If there is no default member, the member at the All level is typically chosen. The default member in this hierarchy (at the All level) has had its AttributeAllMemberName set to All Sales Channels in BIDS. The figure of $80,450,596.98 is for the default measure in the cube (DefaultMeasure property back in BIDS). Here, it is Reseller Sales Amount.

Multiple-Hierarchy Dimension 1/2

Single-hierarchy dimensions are quite rare. Usually, a dimension will have two, and often more, attributes (strictly speaking, we should call them attribute hierarchies). In addition, many dimensions in a cube design have user hierarchies that are composed of two or more attribute hierarchies. We will look at user hierarchies shortly.

Syntax

```
-- multiple-hierarchy dimension
select
[Product] -- dimension
on columns
from
[Adventure Works]
```

Result

```
Executing the query ...
Query (3, 1) The 'Product' dimension contains more than one hierarchy, therefore the hierarchy must be explicitly specified.
..
Execution complete
```

Analysis

This error message is deliberate and informative. To avoid any ambiguity, it is essential that you include the hierarchy name with the dimension name if the dimension has more than one hierarchy. The Product dimension has many attribute and user hierarchies. The next query addresses this problem.

Multiple-Hierarchy Dimension 2/2

The dimension name has now been qualified with a valid hierarchy name. This will eliminate the error message seen in the previous query. In this case, the hierarchy is an attribute hierarchy called Category.

Syntax

```
-- hierarchy specified in multiple-hierarchy dimension
select
[Product].[Category] -- dimension.attribute hierarchy
on columns
from
[Adventure Works]
```

Result

All Products
$80,450,596.98

Analysis

This time the syntax is unambiguous and the MDX returns a cellset consisting of a single cell. The result, once again, depicts the single member at the All level. In BIDS, the AttributeAllMemberName property has been set to All Products. It seems like a good idea to always include both the dimension and the hierarchy name in your queries.

Explicitly Requesting the All Level Member

It's also a good idea to explicitly request the member from the All level too. This was omitted in the previous query. Four queries to try! Hopefully, this one will show you just how it is done—and how it is not done. Some of these queries will work, and one or two may fail.

Syntax

```
select
[Product].[Category].[all] -- dimension.attribute hierarchy
on columns
from
[Adventure Works]
--
select
[Product].[Category].[All] -- dimension.attribute hierarchy
on columns
from
[Adventure Works]
--
```

```
select
[Product].[Category].[(all)] -- dimension.attribute hierarchy
on columns
from
[Adventure Works]
--
select
[Product].[Category].[all products]
-- dimension.attribute hierarchy
on columns
from
[Adventure Works]
```

Result

All Products
$80,450,596.98

Analysis

Not all of the four queries will necessarily produce the result shown. Possibly, the best one to use is [(all)]. One that may cause you the odd headache is [all products]. Firstly, it is not generic and relies on you reproducing exactly the AttributeAllMemberName property that someone else may have set back in BIDS. Secondly, if your SSAS is case-sensitive, it will fail if you get the capitalization wrong. Fortunately, most SSAS installations are case-insensitive. Case-sensitivity, or the lack of it, is a choice made during installation. You can check this by looking at the Language/Collation setting of the SSAS server in SSMS (right-click on your server, choose Properties, and go to the Language/Collation page).

Introducing .members

Dimensions contain one or more hierarchies (zero or more user hierarchies). Hierarchies contain one or more levels (in reality I should say hierarchies contain two or more levels, because there is always, by default, an All level for every hierarchy). Levels contain members. If you are new to multidimensional cubes, that may well sound suitably obscure. It is not absolutely necessary to understand concepts and theory and jargon in order to become productive in MDX. So, maybe, just try the query. Once you do master the concepts, your MDX will become even easier to write and you will be even more productive! The conceptual nature of multidimensional data is beyond the scope of this book. Okay, to really confuse you, because levels have members and hierarchies have levels, then it follows that hierarchies have members too!

One way to reference members is to use the .members syntax. Informally, this is a function. More formally, it is a property function because it is preceded by the dot notation.

The sample query is asking for the members of the Category hierarchy (an attribute hierarchy composed of two levels).

Syntax

```
-- specifying .members
select
[Product].[Category].members
-- dimension.hierarchy.members
on columns
from
[Adventure Works]
```

Result

All Products	Accessories	Bikes	Clothing	Components
$80,450,596.98	$571,297.93	$66,302,381.56	$1,777,840.84	$11,799,076.66

Analysis

[Product].[Category] is the Category attribute of the Product dimension. It is also an attribute hierarchy. So, its members include the All level member as well as the individual category names as members (at the Category level). That's why you get All Products in the result as well as the individual categories. Notice, the All Products member appears first. If you had omitted the .members property function, only All Products would have been returned, as we saw in an earlier query.

More on .members

Here we have one of the most common types of MDX queries. Although it requires more work, it is beginning to look like business intelligence. It makes sense to a business user, hopefully.

You need to see the categories. One of the easiest ways of doing this is to use the .members property function against a level. The following query is asking for the members of the Category level of the Category hierarchy of the Product dimension.

Syntax

```
-- specifying .members for a level
select
```

```
[Product].[Category].[Category].members
-- dimension.hierarchy.level.members
on columns
from
[Adventure Works]
```

Result

Accessories	Bikes	Clothing	Components
$571,297.93	$66,302,381.56	$1,777,840.84	$11,799,076.66

Analysis

[Product] is a dimension. [Product].[Category] is a hierarchy. [Product].[Category] .[Category] is a level. [Product].[Category].[Category].members then returns the members (for example, Accessories and Bikes) of the level.

Note the absence of All Products this time.

If you are completely new to MDX, then references such as [Product].[Product] .[Product] can appear a little strange at first. But, if you understand the rules, it becomes somewhat clearer. [Product].[Product].[Product] means (reading from right to left) the Product level of the Product hierarchy in the Product dimension.

Putting Two Levels Together

The following two queries combine two levels on the Columns axis. Try running them individually. The first query will produce an error. The second query will return some cells.

Syntax

```
-- 2 levels together
select
[Product].[Category].[Category].members,[Product].[Category].[All Products]
on columns
from
[Adventure Works]
-- 2 levels together with {}
select
{[Product].[Category].[Category].members,[Product].[Category].
[All Products]}
on columns
from
[Adventure Works]
```

Result

```
Executing the query ...
Parser: The statement dialect could not be resolved due to ambiguity.

Execution complete
```

Accessories	Bikes	Clothing	Components	All Products
$571,297.93	$66,302,381.56	$1,777,840.84	$11,799,076.66	$80,450,596.98

Analysis

The result of the first query is a very common error message in MDX. To fully understand it, you need to come to grips with some multidimensional concepts. If you prefer not to do so at this stage, simply try the second query with the addition of the { and } delimiters around the Columns axis specification. The { and the } delimiters are known variously as braces, French braces, curly brackets, or often simply and informally as squiggly brackets or squiggles. I guess it depends to some extent on which part of the English-speaking world you live in.

The second query is quite a useful one. It shows each category and then the total for the four categories. You saw similar results in an earlier query, using [Product].[Category] .members, but this one is more flexible. For example, we can position the All Products member after the individual categories.

Why the delimiters? If you are not interested in the theory, then by all means move on. If you do, it is strongly recommended that you return later to this paragraph. A member (of a level/hierarchy/dimension) defines a space within the overall cube space. It points to one or more cells containing one or more measures. In other words, it acts as a coordinate. When a member acts as a coordinate, it is referred to as a *tuple* (pronounce that how you will!). It is one-dimensional. In a multidimensional cube, you also need the coordinates or tuples of all the dimensions to exactly specify a particular cell containing data. In addition, if each cell contains more than one measure, it is also necessary to specify which measure so a cell in the query result shows one and only one number. Consider the Bikes member. It is fairly clear that the cell returned is for Bikes! What is not obvious is for which measure. In our case, because no measure is specified, it uses the default member for the cube, Reseller Sales Amount. Reseller Sales Amount is also a member. It is a member of Measures. Thus, a measure is also a member and a coordinate and a tuple. But, for which year are the sales? After all, no dates are mentioned in the query. When a dimension is not explicitly referenced, the default member is used as an invisible tuple. This applies to all of the dimensions related to a particular measure. Thus, the figure for Bikes is for all time, for all resellers, for all employees, for all promotions, and so on, and so forth. The specification on the Columns axis has two tuples—the first referring to the categories and the second referring to All Products. A specification of an axis is called a *set,* the set being projected along the axis. A single tuple is automatically converted into a set. However, if there is more than one tuple, they must be explicitly converted into a set. The braces, the { and } delimiters, mean explicitly convert to set. If you omit them, MDX gives the ambiguity error message.

Some MDX Shorthand

The query here is a variation on the last query. It demonstrates the use of some very popular shorthand in MDX.

Syntax

```
-- 2 levels short hand
select
{[Product].[Category].[Category],[Product].[Category]}
on columns
from
[Adventure Works]
```

Result

Accessories	Bikes	Clothing	Components	All Products
$571,297.93	$66,302,381.56	$1,777,840.84	$11,799,076.66	$80,450,596.98

Analysis

The results are the same as those from the previous query, but the syntax is shorter. The .members function of the Category level has been omitted, as has the explicit reference to All Products on the Category hierarchy. The behavior of MDX is to return members on a level by default, but to return the default (usually at the All level) member on a hierarchy.

Individual Members

Often, you will want to reference an individual member. There are a number of ways of doing this. Here are four alternatives. Try each one in turn and verify that they all produce the same output.

Syntax

```
-- individual member by key and hierarchy
select
[Product].[Category].&[1]
```

```
on columns
from
[Adventure Works]
-- individual member by name and hierarchy
select
[Product].[Category].[Bikes]
on columns
from
[Adventure Works]
-- individual member by key and level
select
[Product].[Category].[Category].&[1]
on columns
from
[Adventure Works]
-- individual member by name and level
select
[Product].[Category].[Category].[Bikes]
on columns
from
[Adventure Works]
```

Result

Bikes
$66,302,381.56

Analysis

This is a difficult decision. Which one are you going to use when you write your own queries? Note the ampersand (&) in front of the key. When you drag and drop members from the Metadata pane, the key notation is used. Using a key is preferable if you think some members might have duplicate names. For example, although it's unlikely, you might have two categories called Bikes. More likely, you will have two or more customers with the name Smith. Specifying the key value rather than the name value removes any ambiguity. The drawback is that the code is not very readable, and heavy use of keys makes your MDX difficult to understand and debug—especially when you look at it a few days later. Many MDX developers prefer to use the name if they are certain duplicate names do not exist.

The first two examples use only the hierarchy. The second two use the hierarchy and the level. Possibly, using the hierarchy and level together is safer—it is a fully qualified reference. Again, this may be up to personal preference.

Multiple Members

You have just seen how to specify an individual member. Earlier, we looked at how to return a set of members. As you'll recall, there were a total of four product categories. What happens if you want just two or three? The following query demonstrates how to return two product categories.

Syntax

```
-- two members by name
select
{[Product].[Category].[Bikes],[Product].[Category].[Clothing]}
on columns
from
[Adventure Works]
```

Result

Bikes	Clothing
$66,302,381.56	$1,777,840.84

Analysis

Make sure that the two members that are also tuples are converted to a set with the braces delimiters. Otherwise, you will receive an error message. To include a third category, simply add it to the comma-separated list within the braces.

User Hierarchies

The previous queries worked with attribute hierarchies. In reality, your dimensions are likely to contain user hierarchies. User hierarchies are created when dimensions are designed in BIDS. A user hierarchy (often misleadingly called a *multilevel hierarchy*) is a hierarchy that has three or more levels (including the All level at the top), although it is technically possible to create a two-level user hierarchy from a single attribute hierarchy. Attribute hierarchies, on the other hand, typically have two levels (including the All level at the top). It is possible to disable the All level, resulting in a single-level attribute hierarchy, but that is a BIDS design setting and is beyond the scope of an MDX query book.

User hierarchies come in two flavors: natural user hierarchies and unnatural user hierarchies (some people call these *reporting user hierarchies*). Again, this is a BIDS subject area, so we will not go into detail. Whether your hierarchies are natural or unnatural has little relevance on the queries you write, but it may affect the performance of your queries. Natural hierarchies generally return the data for the cells much quicker. For your future reference, natural user hierarchies have attribute relationships set between the attributes (in BIDS) in the levels, and there is a one-to-many relationship from one level to a lower level. Unnatural user hierarchies do not have attribute relationships between the attributes, and often there is a many-to-many relationship between the members of the levels.

Syntax

```
-- user hierarchy
select
[Product].[Product Categories]
on columns
from
[Adventure Works]
```

Result

All Products
$80,450,596.98

Analysis

User hierarchies are represented in the Metadata pane as blue triangles. Many people call them pyramids, which suggest a hierarchical structure. The syntax here is the same as the attribute hierarchy syntax, except it is [Dimension].[User hierarchy] rather than [Dimension].[Attribute hierarchy].

User Hierarchy with .members

The subtle addition of .members gives us a completely different query from the previous one.

Syntax

```
select
[Product].[Product Categories].members
on columns
from
[Adventure Works]
```

Result

All Products	Accessories	Bike Racks	Hitch Rack - 4-Bike
$80,450,596.98	$571,297.93	$197,736.16	$197,736.16

Analysis

Note that I cheated with the screenshot for the result! Your results probably go on and on and require a little scrolling. I am showing the first four columns only. First, there is the All level member, then a category-level member, then a subcategory-level member, then a product-level member. Four levels in four columns. In addition to the All level member, which appears first, as you scroll across you can see every category, every subcategory, and every product. [Dimension].[User hierarchy].members may run very slowly against large dimensions such as customer.

Two Hierarchies from the Same Dimension

Unfortunately, both these queries will fail, and with two different error messages. You can see that they are different if you look closely. At least, you can see what not to do in your own queries!

Syntax

```
-- two hierarchies
select
[Product].[Product Categories],[Product].[Category]
on columns
from
[Adventure Works]
-- two hierarchies with {}
select
{[Product].[Product Categories],[Product].[Category]}
on columns
from
[Adventure Works]
```

Result

```
Executing the query ...
Parser: The statement dialect could not be resolved due to ambiguity.

Execution complete


Executing the query ...
Query (2, 1) Two sets specified in the  function have different dimensionality.

Execution complete
```

Analysis

I guess the lesson here is not to mix and match. MDX does not allow you to have two different hierarchies from the same dimension on the same axis (unless they are in a crossjoin, which is covered shortly). You can, however, have two different hierarchies from the same dimension on two separate axes. This is especially useful with date/time dimensions and is covered later in the chapter.

Transposing Columns onto Rows

The Product Categories hierarchy had a lot of columns, as you saw earlier. Often, it is easier to scroll down rather than across, and it is a bit easier to read. These two queries attempt to project the set of members onto the Rows axis.

Syntax

```
-- rows instead of columns
select
[Product].[Product Categories].members
on rows
from
[Adventure Works]
-- try again
select
{} on columns,
[Product].[Product Categories].members
on rows
from
[Adventure Works]
```

Result

```
Executing the query ...
Query (2, 1) Axis numbers specified in a query must be sequentially specified, and cannot contain gaps.

Execution complete
```

Analysis

The error from the first query is stating that you can't have a Rows axis unless you have a Columns axis first.

The second query is going to produce a lot of rows! Again, I used a partial screenshot for the result. It does demonstrate a useful technique for incrementally developing your queries. The braces ({}) generate an empty set on the Columns axis—very handy when you want to get the rows right first, before you concentrate on the columns.

Adding a Measure Explicitly

It's sometimes a good idea to include a measure explicitly on the query axes. If you don't, in absence of a measure in the Where clause, the default measure is used. What's worse is that an end user may not know about default measures. To make it abundantly clear what the figures are, consider adding one or more measures to one of the axes.

Syntax

```
-- once more on rows with measures dimension on columns
select
[Measures].[Reseller Sales Amount] on columns,
[Product].[Product Categories].members
on rows
from
[Adventure Works]
```

Result

	Reseller Sales Amount
All Products	$80,450,596.98
Accessories	$571,297.93
Bike Racks	$197,736.16
Hitch Rack - 4-Bike	$197,736.16

Analysis

Yes, another partial screenshot. The empty set on the Columns axis in the last query has been replaced by Reseller Sales Amount. Some of our queries are getting to be quite useful.

A short conceptual point: Reseller Sales Amount is a member. It is also a tuple because it points somewhere. It is also a set because it has been projected along a query axis—and that qualifies it as a dimension! Yes, Measures is a dimension too, even if it's based on a nondimensional relational table (the fact table). It is a dimension with no hierarchies and no levels as such. Therefore, the syntax is [Dimension].[Member] or [Measures].[Reseller Sales Amount] in this example.

Two Dimensions on Two Axes

Now let's get some practice putting two dimensions on two axes. Strictly speaking, we should say putting two non-measure dimensions on two axes. The Date dimension is on the Columns axis, and the Product dimension is on the Rows axis.

Syntax

```
-- 2 different non-measure dimensions on 2 axes
select
[Date].[Calendar].[Calendar Year]
on columns,
[Product].[Product Categories].[Category]
on rows
from
[Adventure Works]
-- and again
select
[Product].[Product Categories].[Category]
on columns,
[Date].[Calendar].[Calendar Year]
on rows
from
[Adventure Works]
```

Result

	CY 2001	CY 2002	CY 2003	CY 2004	CY 2006
Accessories	$20,235.36	$92,735.35	$296,532.88	$161,794.33	(null)
Bikes	$7,395,348.63	$19,956,014.67	$25,551,775.07	$13,399,243.18	(null)
Clothing	$34,376.34	$485,587.15	$871,864.19	$386,013.16	(null)
Components	$615,474.98	$3,610,092.47	$5,482,497.29	$2,091,011.92	(null)

	Accessories	Bikes	Clothing	Components
CY 2001	$20,235.36	$7,395,348.63	$34,376.34	$615,474.98
CY 2002	$92,735.35	$19,956,014.67	$485,587.15	$3,610,092.47
CY 2003	$296,532.88	$25,551,775.07	$871,864.19	$5,482,497.29
CY 2004	$161,794.33	$13,399,243.18	$386,013.16	$2,091,011.92
CY 2006	(null)	(null)	(null)	(null)

Analysis

Here we have two ways of looking at the same cells. The effect is achieved simply by transposing (or *pivoting*, hence the name pivot table) the sets on the two axes.

Incidentally, many end users prefer to see dates on columns rather than on rows, so maybe the first query looks a little better?

Same Non-measure Dimension on Two Axes

Quite a common request is to see monthly figures compared from year to year, with the Years on the Columns axis and the Months on the Rows axis. You might be tempted to try a query like the following.

Syntax

```
-- same non-measure dimension on 2 axes
select
[Date].[Calendar].[Calendar Year]
on columns,
[Date].[Calendar].[Month]
on rows
from
[Adventure Works]
```

Result

```
Executing the query ...
The Calendar hierarchy already appears in the Axis0 axis.

Execution complete
```

Analysis

Unfortunately, it simply doesn't work. You can't have the same hierarchy from the same dimension on more than one axis. Fortunately, the next query has a solution.

Same Non-measure Dimension on Two Axes with Differing Hierarchies

Here is the correct way to solve this situation. This time there is no error message, and we are displaying useful intelligence to the end user.

Syntax

```
-- comparing months across years
select
[Date].[Calendar].[Calendar Year]
```

```
on columns,
[Date].[Month of Year].[Month of Year]
on rows
from
[Adventure Works]
```

Result

	CY 2001	CY 2002	CY 2003
January	(null)	$713,116.69	$1,317,541.83
February	(null)	$1,900,788.93	$2,384,846.59
March	(null)	$1,455,280.41	$1,563,955.08
April	(null)	$882,899.94	$1,865,278.43
May	(null)	$2,269,116.71	$2,880,752.68
June	(null)	$1,001,803.77	$1,987,872.71
July	$489,328.58	$2,393,689.53	$2,665,650.54
August	$1,538,408.31	$3,601,190.71	$4,212,971.51
September	$1,165,897.08	$2,885,359.20	$4,047,574.04
October	$844,721.00	$1,802,154.21	$2,282,115.88
November	$2,324,135.80	$3,053,816.33	$3,483,161.40
December	$1,702,944.54	$2,185,213.21	$3,510,948.73

Analysis

The resultant screenshot depicts the 12 months of the year, but only shows a sample of the years. Note, for example, how easy it is to compare December CY 2001 to December CY 2002.

Years and Months on the Same Axis

Maybe you don't want years and months on two axes. Maybe you prefer years and months on the same axis. Here are two attempts.

Syntax

```
-- months by year again, different hierarchies
select
[Measures].[Internet Sales Amount]
on columns,
{[Date].[Calendar].[Calendar Year],[Date].[Month of Year].[Month of Year]}
on rows
from
[Adventure Works]
-- months by year again, same hierarchy
select
[Measures].[Internet Sales Amount]
```

```
on columns,
{[Date].[Calendar].[Calendar Year],[Date].[Calendar].[Month]}
on rows
from
[Adventure Works]
```

Result

```
Executing the query ...
Query (4, 1) Two sets specified in the  function have different dimensionality.

Execution complete
```

	Internet Sales Amount
CY 2001	$3,266,373.66
CY 2002	$6,530,343.53
CY 2003	$9,791,060.30
CY 2004	$9,770,899.74
CY 2006	(null)
July 2001	$473,388.16
August 2001	$506,191.69
September 2001	$473,943.03
October 2001	$513,329.47
November 2001	$543,993.41
December 2001	$755,527.89
January 2002	$596,746.56
February 2002	$550,816.69
March 2002	$644,135.20
April 2002	$663,692.29
May 2002	$673,556.20
June 2002	$676,763.65
July 2002	$500,365.16

Analysis

The first query returns an error because we are trying to use two different hierarchies from the same dimension on the same axis. In the second query, the same hierarchy is used twice, albeit at two different levels. It works, but just barely. However, the separation of the years from the months makes the result difficult to read. There must be a better way.

Years and Months on the Same Axis with a Crossjoin

All things are possible in MDX (well, mostly). Enter what is one of the most popular techniques in MDX—the crossjoin. This is a very powerful feature, so it makes sense to understand how (and how not) to use it.

Syntax

```
-- crossjoin working
select
[Measures].[Internet Sales Amount]
on columns,
crossjoin([Date].[Calendar].[Calendar Year],
[Date].[Month of Year].[Month of Year])
on rows
from
[Adventure Works]
-- crossjoin not working
select
[Measures].[Internet Sales Amount]
on columns,
crossjoin([Date].[Calendar].[Calendar Year],[Date].[Calendar].[Month])
on rows
from
[Adventure Works]
```

Result

		Internet Sales Amount
CY 2001	July	$473,388.16
CY 2001	August	$506,191.69
CY 2001	September	$473,943.03
CY 2001	October	$513,329.47
CY 2001	November	$543,993.41
CY 2001	December	$755,527.89
CY 2002	January	$596,746.56
CY 2002	February	$550,816.69
CY 2002	March	$644,135.20
CY 2002	April	$663,692.29
CY 2002	May	$673,556.20
CY 2002	June	$676,763.65
CY 2002	July	$500,365.16

```
Executing the query ...
Query (4, 1) The Calendar hierarchy is used more than once in the Crossjoin function.

Execution complete
```

Analysis

Crossjoin is a function. More specifically, it is a method function. Property functions such as .members use the dot notation and follow the object (for example, a level). Method functions precede the object (for example, a set of members).

The first try at Crossjoin proved successful. The second attempt produced an error. There is a fundamental rule about Crossjoin: If you crossjoin two sets of members from the same dimension, the two sets must be based on different hierarchies within the same dimension. You can even crossjoin two different dimensions.

Introducing a Second Measure into the Crossjoin

The Crossjoin query is getting more interesting.

Syntax

```
-- adding another measure
select
{[Measures].[Internet Sales Amount],[Measures].[Reseller Sales Amount]}
on columns,
crossjoin([Date].[Calendar].[Calendar Year],
[Date].[Month of Year].[Month of Year])
on rows
from
[Adventure Works]
```

Result

		Internet Sales Amount	Reseller Sales Amount
CY 2001	July	$473,388.16	$489,328.58
CY 2001	August	$506,191.69	$1,538,408.31
CY 2001	September	$473,943.03	$1,165,897.08
CY 2001	October	$513,329.47	$844,721.00
CY 2001	November	$543,993.41	$2,324,135.80
CY 2001	December	$755,527.89	$1,702,944.54
CY 2002	January	$596,746.56	$713,116.69
CY 2002	February	$550,816.69	$1,900,788.93
CY 2002	March	$644,135.20	$1,455,280.41
CY 2002	April	$663,692.29	$882,899.94
CY 2002	May	$673,556.20	$2,269,116.71
CY 2002	June	$676,763.65	$1,001,803.77
CY 2002	July	$500,365.16	$2,393,689.53

Analysis

This is a fairly simple change. Because we have two measures on the Columns axis, they must be delimited with braces.

A Second Crossjoin on a Second Axis

If you have two axes, you can have a separate crossjoin on each axis.

Syntax

```
-- crossjoin on 2 axes
select
crossjoin([Product].[Product Categories].[Category],
{[Measures].[Internet Sales Amount],[Measures].[Reseller Sales Amount]})
on columns,
crossjoin([Date].[Calendar].[Calendar Year],
[Date].[Month of Year].[Month of Year])
on rows
from
[Adventure Works]
```

Result

		Accessories	Accessories	Bikes	Bikes
		Internet Sales Amount	Reseller Sales Amount	Internet Sales Amount	Reseller Sales Amount
CY 2001	July	(null)	$1,695.67	$473,388.16	$453,231.80
CY 2001	August	(null)	$3,593.20	$506,191.69	$1,413,253.52
CY 2001	September	(null)	$3,250.03	$473,943.03	$1,054,995.97
CY 2001	October	(null)	$1,937.90	$513,329.47	$777,394.97
CY 2001	November	(null)	$5,490.73	$543,993.41	$2,152,858.49
CY 2001	December	(null)	$4,267.84	$755,527.89	$1,543,613.88
CY 2002	January	(null)	$585.41	$596,746.56	$687,178.08
CY 2002	February	(null)	$2,159.96	$550,816.69	$1,814,374.32
CY 2002	March	(null)	$2,200.33	$644,135.20	$1,375,940.84
CY 2002	April	(null)	$1,776.41	$663,692.29	$813,847.26
CY 2002	May	(null)	$5,577.84	$673,556.20	$2,082,726.08
CY 2002	June	(null)	$4,279.54	$676,763.65	$849,118.85
CY 2002	July	(null)	$10,477.61	$500,365.16	$1,801,927.63

Analysis

This is building nicely. Once again, the braces delimiters around the two measures are important.

Crossjoin on Two Separate Non-measure Dimensions

Not only can you crossjoin the same dimension (provided you use differing hierarchies) or crossjoin using the measures dimension, you can also crossjoin two different non-measure dimensions.

Syntax

```
--
select
crossjoin([Sales Territory].[Sales Territory].[Country],
[Product].[Product Categories].[Category])
on columns,
crossjoin([Date].[Calendar].[Calendar Year],
[Date].[Month of Year].[Month of Year])
on rows
from
[Adventure Works]
```

Result

		Canada	Canada	Canada	Canada	United States
		Accessories	Bikes	Clothing	Components	Accessories
CY 2001	July	$302.80	$99,240.99	$736.11	$15,080.99	$1,392.87
CY 2001	August	$847.83	$293,581.57	$1,304.86	$21,246.81	$2,745.36
CY 2001	September	$908.39	$182,503.16	$976.75	$21,252.57	$2,341.63
CY 2001	October	$524.85	$210,463.22	$933.18	$22,985.99	$1,413.06
CY 2001	November	$1,413.06	$356,669.19	$1,919.16	$21,805.08	$4,077.67
CY 2001	December	$1,150.63	$228,263.14	$2,043.27	$27,205.85	$3,117.21
CY 2002	January	$201.87	$154,028.98	$330.92	$9,218.07	$383.54
CY 2002	February	$645.97	$257,729.62	$1,366.45	$16,889.11	$1,513.99
CY 2002	March	$403.73	$317,344.58	$840.72	$16,755.45	$1,796.60
CY 2002	April	$363.36	$204,146.65	$804.17	$22,753.56	$1,413.06
CY 2002	May	$1,056.06	$351,100.57	$2,170.06	$30,315.92	$4,521.78
CY 2002	June	$1,069.88	$153,851.87	$1,904.67	$21,155.11	$3,209.65
CY 2002	July	$2,502.00	$479,438.41	$16,224.33	$139,950.45	$6,531.56

Analysis

The result set is getting quite large. The screenshot shows only a small part of it. It includes, for example, Accessories for Canada and Accessories for the United States.

A More Complex Crossjoin

Yes, you guessed! You can have crossjoins within crossjoins. A crossjoin effectively allows you to place two dimensions on one axis (if the sets of members are from two dimensions). You can think of them as nested dimensions. A crossjoin on a crossjoin allows three dimensions on one axis.

Syntax

```
-- a more complex crossjoin
select
crossjoin([Sales Territory].[Sales Territory]
.[Country],crossjoin([Product].[Product Categories].[Category],
{[Measures].[Internet Order Count],[Measures].[Reseller Order Count]}))
on columns,
crossjoin([Date].[Calendar].[Calendar Year],
[Date].[Month of Year].[Month of Year])
on rows
from
[Adventure Works]
```

Result

		France	France	France	France
		Accessories	Accessories	Bikes	Bikes
		Internet Order Count	Reseller Order Count	Internet Order Count	Reseller Order Count
CY 2003	July	41	3	54	2
CY 2003	August	114	7	55	16
CY 2003	September	135	4	61	6
CY 2003	October	110	2	44	3
CY 2003	November	114	7	61	16
CY 2003	December	179	2	115	7
CY 2004	January	126	3	66	3
CY 2004	February	155	3	95	16
CY 2004	March	162	3	81	6
CY 2004	April	163	2	96	4
CY 2004	May	156	7	102	16
CY 2004	June	161	3	120	6
CY 2004	July	68	(null)	(null)	(null)

Analysis

Rather a lot of results. You may have to scroll to see the cells shown in the screenshot. Crossjoins within crossjoins are a way of displaying multiple dimensions in two-dimensional output, such as the query editor's Results pane, an Excel worksheet, or an SSRS report.

A word of caution: Too many crossjoins of sets with large numbers of members will return thousands, possibly millions, of cells. You will need to do a lot of scrolling to see all the data. Also, you may find that some queries take a little while to run.

When you are designing complex crossjoins, it is a good idea to get the innermost crossjoin working first, before you build the outer crossjoin on the inner crossjoin.

Alternative Crossjoin Syntax 1/2

A crossjoin does not always require the Crossjoin function. Here is an alternative syntax for a crossjoin. This might prove useful if you inherit MDX queries written by others. Some people use this syntax—take a look at the specification of the Rows axis.

Syntax

```
-- alternative crossjoin syntax 1/2
select
crossjoin([Sales Territory].[Sales Territory].[Country],
[Product].[Product Categories].[Category],
{[Measures].[Internet Order Count],[Measures].[Reseller Order Count]})
on columns,
([Date].[Calendar].[Calendar Year],[Date].[Month of Year].[Month of Year])
on rows
from
[Adventure Works]
```

Result

		France	France	France	France
		Accessories	Accessories	Bikes	Bikes
		Internet Order Count	Reseller Order Count	Internet Order Count	Reseller Order Count
CY 2003	July	41	3	54	2
CY 2003	August	114	7	55	16
CY 2003	September	135	4	61	6
CY 2003	October	110	2	44	3
CY 2003	November	114	7	61	16
CY 2003	December	179	2	115	7
CY 2004	January	126	3	66	3
CY 2004	February	155	3	95	16
CY 2004	March	162	3	81	6
CY 2004	April	163	2	96	4
CY 2004	May	156	7	102	16
CY 2004	June	161	3	120	6
CY 2004	July	68	(null)	(null)	(null)

Analysis

The Crossjoin function has been removed from the Rows axis specification. This will work provided the two sets are separated by a comma and enclosed within parentheses.

Alternative Crossjoin Syntax 2/2

You may also meet this form of the syntax. Once again, the Rows axis specification has been changed.

Syntax

```
-- alternative crossjoin syntax 2/2
select
crossjoin([Sales Territory].[Sales Territory].[Country],[Product].
[Product Categories].[Category],
{[Measures].[Internet Order Count],[Measures].[Reseller Order Count]})
on columns,
[Date].[Calendar].[Calendar Year]*[Date].[Month of Year].[Month of Year]
on rows
from
[Adventure Works]
```

Result

		France	France	France	France
		Accessories	Accessories	Bikes	Bikes
		Internet Order Count	Reseller Order Count	Internet Order Count	Reseller Order Count
CY 2003	July	41	3	54	2
CY 2003	August	114	7	55	16
CY 2003	September	135	4	61	6
CY 2003	October	110	2	44	3
CY 2003	November	114	7	61	16
CY 2003	December	179	2	115	7
CY 2004	January	126	3	66	3
CY 2004	February	155	3	95	16
CY 2004	March	162	3	81	6
CY 2004	April	163	2	96	4
CY 2004	May	156	7	102	16
CY 2004	June	161	3	120	6
CY 2004	July	68	(null)	(null)	(null)

Analysis

Because a crossjoin is essentially a multiplication operation, you can also use the multiplication symbol between the two sets of members.

More on Members

In a sense, crossjoins give you all possible combinations of members. Many, many cells can be returned. Sometimes, this is what you want. However, often you will want only a few cells. If you know the members (tuples) that point to those cells, you can explicitly use just those members in your query. Take a look at the members on the Columns axis.

Syntax

```
-- members from different levels of same hierarchy
select
{[Date].[Calendar].[Calendar Semester].[H1 CY 2003],
[Date].[Calendar].[Calendar Semester].[H2 CY 2003],
[Date].[Calendar].[Calendar Year].[CY 2003]}
on columns,
{[Sales Territory].[Sales Territory].[Group],
[Sales Territory].[Sales Territory]}
on rows
from
[Adventure Works]
```

Result

	H1 CY 2003	H2 CY 2003	CY 2003
Europe	$1,135,631.40	$4,497,185.16	$5,632,816.55
NA	(null)	(null)	(null)
North America	$10,864,615.93	$14,857,805.98	$25,722,421.91
Pacific	(null)	$847,430.96	$847,430.96
All Sales Territories	$12,000,247.33	$20,202,422.10	$32,202,669.43

Analysis

This is a little different from a crossjoin. Incidentally, there are entries on the rows for NA and North America. (NA does not mean North America!)

Chapter 3

Families and Friends: Navigating Dimensions

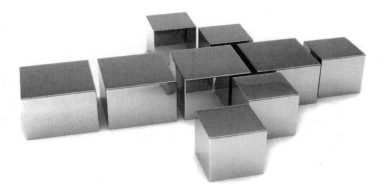

I n this chapter, we explore moving up and down and across dimensions and hierarchies. The general term for doing this is *navigation*. MDX allows you to navigate both horizontally and vertically. MDX (unlike SQL) is positionally aware—it knows where you are in the cube and can help you in your navigation.

▶   **Key concepts**   Finding dimension members that have some relationship to a particular member, using ranges

▶   **Keywords**   .children, Descendants, Exists, .parent, Ancestor, Ascendants, Hierarchize, .siblings, .firstchild, .firstsibling, .lastchild, .lastsibling, Cousin, .lead, .lag, Head, Tail, .prevmember, .nextmember

Dimensions Have Members

Dimensions have members. For example, the country France is a member of the Customer dimension. The property function to enumerate members is .members.

Syntax

```
-- dimension members
select
[Customer].members
on columns
from
[Adventure Works]
```

Result

```
Executing the query ...
Query (2, 1) The 'Customer' dimension contains more than one hierarchy, therefore the hierarchy must be explicitly specified.
Execution complete
```

Analysis

If, as is usual, a dimension contains more than one hierarchy (attribute and user hierarchies), then you can't use .members to list all the members in the dimension. Anyway, listing all the members of a large dimension might easily return millions of members. It makes more sense to divide up the dimension. Using hierarchies enables you to do this.

Hierarchies Have Members

Because the hierarchy (Customer Geography) is explicitly contained in the query, it doesn't matter that the dimension (Customer) has more than one hierarchy.

Syntax

```
-- hierarchy members
select
[Measures].[Internet Sales Amount]
on columns,
[Customer].[Customer Geography].members
on rows
from
[Adventure Works]
```

Result

	Internet Sales Amount
All Customers	$29,358,677.22
Australia	$9,061,000.58
New South Wales	$3,934,485.73
Alexandria	(null)
2015	(null)
Coffs Harbour	$235,454.97
2450	$235,454.97
Adriana Smith	$5,333.25
Aimee Guo	$77.27
Allison R. Young	$39.98
Ann A. Sara	$39.98

Analysis

This is a pretty big hierarchy. It may take a second or two for the results to be returned. Only a very small section is shown in the screenshot. Perhaps the lesson to learn here is that dimensions have members, dimensions have hierarchies, and hierarchies have members. The members of a hierarchy are arranged in levels; therefore, it follows that levels also have members.

Levels Have Members

Running this query proves that levels have members. We are using the Country level of the Customer Geography hierarchy of the Customer dimension.

Syntax

```
-- level members
select
[Measures].[Internet Sales Amount]
on columns,
[Customer].[Customer Geography].[Country].members
on rows
from
[Adventure Works]
```

Result

	Internet Sales Amount
Australia	$9,061,000.58
Canada	$1,977,844.86
France	$2,644,017.71
Germany	$2,894,312.34
United Kingdom	$3,391,712.21
United States	$9,389,789.51

Analysis

Hopefully we have established that levels have members. Hierarchies have members, with a level containing a subset of the hierarchy members. Dimensions have members, with a hierarchy containing a subset of the dimension members. At the risk of sounding a little repetitive, dimensions and hierarchies and levels all have members. In addition, dimensions have hierarchies, and hierarchies have levels. This discussion is preliminary to the queries in this chapter that are concerned with navigating to members using levels and hierarchies. I wonder if members have members as well?

Do Member Have Members?

Let's go down another tier. The query has been extended from the last one to include a member (France).

Syntax

```
-- member members
select
[Measures].[Internet Sales Amount]
on columns,
[Customer].[Customer Geography].[Country].[France].members
on rows
from
[Adventure Works]
```

Result

```
Executing the query ...
Query (4, 1) The MEMBERS function expects a level expression for the 1 argument. A member expression was used.
Execution complete
```

Analysis

The gist of the error message is that you can't use the .members function on a member. Members don't have members. Members have something different, and they are called children.

Members Have Children

The .members function has been replaced with .children.

Syntax

```
-- children
select
[Measures].[Internet Sales Amount]
on columns,
[Customer].[Customer Geography].[Country].[France].children
on rows
from
[Adventure Works]
```

Result

	Internet Sales Amount
Charente-Maritime	$34,441.73
Essonne	$279,297.18
Garonne (Haute)	$54,641.72
Gers	(null)
Hauts de Seine	$263,416.19
Loir et Cher	$21,473.74
Loiret	$91,562.91
Moselle	$94,046.23
Nord	$391,400.20
Pas de Calais	$11,342.92
Seine (Paris)	$539,725.80
Seine et Marne	$109,735.24
Seine Saint Denis	$379,479.75
Somme	$29,555.28
Val de Marne	$28,478.12
Val d'Oise	$46,755.90
Yveline	$268,664.80

Analysis

Members have children. Members don't have members. To say that members have children is true up to a point. The children of France, for example, include Yveline. France is at the Country level, and Yveline is at the State-Province level. You can check this by expanding the Customer Geography hierarchy pyramid in the Metadata pane. The children of France do not include Paris. This is because Paris is at the City level of the hierarchy. Paris is a grandchild, rather than a child, of France. Then we could go down to the next level (Postal Code) and even to the next level (Customer). The Customer level is the lowest level in the hierarchy—it's called the leaf level. You can't drill any further down. Therefore, members of the Customer level don't have children—but they do have a parent!

So how do we get down to Paris from France? How do we jump a level? Jumping up and down and across hierarchies is called *navigation*.

How to Get to Paris from France

You just saw .children being used to return the state-provinces of France. Paris at the City level is one level below that. This query tries .children.children.

Syntax

```
-- French cities
select
[Measures].[Internet Sales Amount]
on columns,
[Customer].[Customer Geography].[Country].[France].children.children
on rows
from
[Adventure Works]
```

Result

```
Executing the query ...
Query (4, 1) The CHILDREN function expects a member expression for the 1 argument. A tuple set expression was used.

Execution complete
```

Analysis

The error message indicates that children don't have children, only members have children. So, we can't use .children.children to jump to Paris from France. And, unfortunately, there is no .grandchildren function. But, you can use Descendants.

Traversing Levels with Descendants

Here we have the syntax to show the grandchildren of a member. The Descendants function is part of the Rows axis specification in this example.

Syntax

```
-- grandchildren with descendants
select
[Measures].[Internet Sales Amount]
on columns,
descendants([Customer].[Customer Geography].[Country].[France],[Customer]
.[Customer Geography].[City])
on rows
from
[Adventure Works]
```

Result

	Internet Sales Amount
Roncq	$38,304.87
Roubaix	$86,282.63
Villeneuve-d'Ascq	$89,136.45
Boulogne-sur-Mer	$11,342.92
Paris	$539,725.80
Lieusaint	$57,094.80
Roissy en Brie	$52,640.44
Bobigny	$90,204.45
Drancy	$56,031.38
Pantin	$77,603.76
Saint-Denis	$63,782.59
Tremblay-en-France	$91,857.57
Saint Ouen	$29,555.28
Orly	$28,478.12
Cergy	$46,755.90
Chatou	$89,830.20
Saint Germain en Laye	$76,177.34
Versailles	$102,657.25

Analysis

Now you have Paris starting from France. You may have to scroll down a little to see Paris. The Descendants syntax means "find the cities at the City level (second parameter of the function) of France at the Country level (first parameter)."

More on Descendants

The previous query found grandchildren—it skipped the State-Province level. This time we are going to skip the Postal Code level as well. In effect, you are retrieving the great-great-grandchildren of France.

Syntax

```
-- or even great-great grandchildren
select
[Measures].[Internet Sales Amount]
on columns,
descendants([Customer].[Customer Geography].[Country].[France],[Customer]
.[Customer Geography].[Customer])
on rows
from
[Adventure Works]
```

Result

	Internet Sales Amount
Brad Nath	$48.97
Bridget C. Nath	$1,560.43
Chelsea Jordan	$1,735.98
Clayton Zhang	$2,049.10
Colin R. Wang	$47.97
Craig R. Gill	$23.78
Darren A. Ruiz	$43.46
Dominic A. Garcia	$1,382.97
Edwin Zhou	$2,753.82
Jon Cai	$88.97
Julie Pal	$2,778.52
Katie Shan	$8.99

Analysis

The result is from the Results pane of the query editor window. Sometimes it's helpful to know just how many cells you have. If you click the Messages tab, it will tell you that there are more than 1,800 rows. We have over 1,800 customers in France. One of those customers is named Crystal Zheng—trust me? I don't expect you to scroll through over 1,800 customers to find her! Instead, in the next query, we'll prove she exists. If she does, then she will serve us well in subsequent navigation queries. Descendants is returning members at the Customer level (second parameter to the function) that belong to France at the Country level (first parameter in the function).

Proving a Member (Crystal Zheng) Exists 1/3

Before we use one customer (Crystal Zheng) as a starting point for some navigation queries, it's worth checking to see if she exists. This is very important—if you start from the wrong place, you won't be able to reach your destination. Here are three queries—they all do pretty much the same thing. There is a deliberate typo in all three—Crystal Zhen (who does not exist) rather than Crystal Zheng (who might exist).

Syntax

```
-- checking Crystal Zheng exists 1/3 as Crystal Zhen!
-- informally
select
[Customer].[Customer Geography].[Customer].[Crystal Zhen]
-- deliberate typo
on columns
from
[Adventure Works]
-- more formally
select
exists([Customer].[Customer Geography].[Customer].[Crystal Zhen],
[Customer].[Customer Geography].members)
-- deliberate typo
on columns
from
[Adventure Works]
-- more formally without Customer level
select
exists([Customer].[Customer Geography].[Crystal Zhen],
[Customer].[Customer Geography].members)
-- deliberate typo
on columns
from
[Adventure Works]
```

Result

Analysis

No results at all! The preceding "Result" section is intentionally blank. Typically, when you specify a member that does not exist, your Results pane is empty. The third query might prove particularly useful. You can use this form when you don't even know the level (but know the hierarchy) at which the member might exist. The second and third queries incorporate the Exists function.

Proving a Member (Crystal Zheng) Exists 2/3

This time, we try without the typo, and Crystal Zheng is entered correctly. Again, there are three queries. All three return the same result.

Syntax

```
-- checking Crystal Zheng exists 2/3 as Crystal Zheng
-- informally
select
[Customer].[Customer Geography].[Customer].[Crystal Zheng]
on columns
from
[Adventure Works]
-- more formally
select
exists([Customer].[Customer Geography].[Customer].
[Crystal Zheng],[Customer].[Customer Geography].members)
on columns
from
[Adventure Works]
-- more formally without Customer level
select
exists([Customer].[Customer Geography].[Crystal Zheng],
[Customer].[Customer Geography].members)
on columns
from
[Adventure Works]
```

Result

Crystal Zheng
$80,450,596.98

Analysis

This looks more promising. Crystal Zheng appears in the Results pane. Once more, the third variation on the query is useful if you don't know at which level of the hierarchy she lives. (Note that she appears to be a very good customer!)

Proving a Member (Crystal Zheng) Exists 3/3

Here are another three queries (the final ones) in our pursuit of Crystal Zheng. Is she really one of our top spending customers at over $80 million dollars (that's a lot of bikes)?

Syntax

```
-- checking Crystal Zheng exists -3/3
-- but all good customers!
select
[Measures].[Reseller Sales Amount]
on columns,
[Customer].[Customer Geography].[Customer].members
on rows
from
[Adventure Works]
-- better
select
[Measures].[Internet Sales Amount]
on columns,
[Customer].[Customer Geography].[Customer].members
on rows
from
[Adventure Works]
-- only Crystal Zheng
select
[Measures].[Internet Sales Amount]
on columns,
[Customer].[Customer Geography].[Customer].[Crystal Zheng]
on rows
from
[Adventure Works]
```

Result

	Reseller Sales Amount
Adriana Smith	$80,450,596.98
Aimee Guo	$80,450,596.98
Allison R. Young	$80,450,596.98
Ann A. Sara	$80,450,596.98
Antonio G. Patterson	$80,450,596.98
Ariana Stewart	$80,450,596.98
Arthur Kapoor	$80,450,596.98

	Internet Sales Amount
Adriana Smith	$5,333.25
Aimee Guo	$77.27
Allison R. Young	$39.98
Ann A. Sara	$39.98
Antonio G. Patterson	$8,068.03
Ariana Stewart	$6,070.59
Arthur Kapoor	$23.97

	Internet Sales Amount
Crystal Zheng	$60.47

Analysis

Hey, all our customers are really good. Everyone spends over $80 million! Or so the result of the first query seems to suggest. Unfortunately, as you might imagine, the results are spurious. Repeating figures like this is an indication that, even though the members exist, the measure shown in the cells is not a valid measure for the members. The default measure (the one shown in the first result set) is Reseller Sales Amount. In BIDS, this measure is a part of the Reseller Sales measure group, which is not linked to the Customer dimension. These links are set through the Dimension Usage tab of your cube design. (Cube design in BIDS is beyond the scope of this book—you can write effective MDX without a knowledge of BIDS. However, be aware of the problem of repeating figures.) But the Customer dimension is related to the Internet Sales measure group, of which Internet Sales Amount is a measure. The second query is showing valid results. The third and final query demonstrates that Crystal Zheng not only exists but the figure for her Internet Sales Amount is real ($60 rather than $80 million).

Children of Crystal Zheng

A little earlier you saw the .children function. Let's try it out for Crystal Zheng.

Syntax

```
-- children of Crystal Zheng
select
[Measures].[Internet Sales Amount]
on columns,
[Customer].[Customer Geography].[Customer].[Crystal Zheng].children
on rows
from
[Adventure Works]
```

Result

Internet Sales Amount

Analysis

The result is simply a caption, with no cells containing data. The query has returned no valid members. This indicates that Crystal Zheng does indeed have no children. Do you recall that earlier we said that members have children? Well, this is only potentially so. Members of the lowest level of a hierarchy do not have children. Members at the lowest level are called the *leaf-level members*.

Parent of Crystal Zheng

The next level up in Customer Geography is Postal Code. MDX has a .parent function that enables us to work out the postal code for Crystal Zheng.

Syntax

```
-- parent of Crystal Zheng
select
[Measures].[Internet Sales Amount]
on columns,
[Customer].[Customer Geography].[Customer].[Crystal Zheng].parent
on rows
from
[Adventure Works]
```

Result

	Internet Sales Amount
78000	$102,657.25

Analysis

Her postal code is 78000. Notice the measure is no longer $60—the figure shown is the total sales for all customers with a postal code of 78000.

Grandparent

The next level up is City. Sadly, there is no .grandparent function. Instead try .parent .parent.

Syntax

```
--parent.parent (grandparent)
select
[Measures].[Internet Sales Amount]
on columns,
[Customer].[Customer Geography].[Customer].[Crystal Zheng].parent.parent
on rows
from
[Adventure Works]
```

Result

Analysis

Crystal Zheng lives in Versailles. But, this time, the measure has not changed in value. It's the same as the total at the Postal Code level in the previous query. This would seem to suggest that either Versailles has only one postal code (78000) or that it has only one (78000) with any sales. Now that you know how, you could test this by using .children on Versailles.

Great-Grandparent

And we can keep going. This one takes us to the State-Province level. The query has three .parent functions.

Syntax

```
-- (great-grandparent)
select
[Measures].[Internet Sales Amount]
on columns,
```

```
[Customer].[Customer Geography].[Customer].[Crystal Zheng].parent.parent
.parent
on rows
from
[Adventure Works]
```

Result

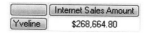

Analysis

As you probably knew already, Versailles is in Yveline. I didn't know that until I wrote the query! Crystal Zheng's province is Yveline. Navigation is extremely valuable when you don't know the relationships between members at different levels.

Back to France

This time, there are four .parent functions for you. The typing gets a little tedious. Shortly, we will see how to eliminate all this typing.

Syntax

```
-- more .parents!
select
[Measures].[Internet Sales Amount]
on columns,
[Customer].[Customer Geography].[Customer].
[Crystal Zheng].parent.parent.parent.parent
on rows
from
[Adventure Works]
```

Result

Analysis

Yveline is in France. Earlier, we started from France and moved down the hierarchy (drilled down) to Crystal Zheng. Now we have started from Crystal Zheng and moved up the hierarchy (drilled up) to France.

Last of the Parents

Here's the last of our .parent queries. We can go no further with this hierarchy. The first query here reaches the top. The second query goes over the top.

Syntax

```
-- right to the top
select
[Measures].[Internet Sales Amount]
on columns,
[Customer].[Customer Geography].[Customer].[Crystal Zheng].parent.parent
.parent.parent.parent
on rows
from
[Adventure Works]
--off the scale up
select
[Measures].[Internet Sales Amount]
on columns,
[Customer].[Customer Geography].[Customer].
[Crystal Zheng].parent.parent.parent.parent.parent.parent
on rows
from
[Adventure Works]
```

Result

Analysis

Our first result set (cellset) has reached the very top of the hierarchy, the apex of the pyramid, and returns data for the All level member (All Customers). The second set of results has no cells. There is no higher member than the All level member in any hierarchy.

Ancestor Rather Than .parent

We need a respite from all those .parents. Fortunately, there is a shorthand—it's the Ancestor method function. Two variations of the syntax are illustrated here. Both produce the same result.

Syntax

```
-- ancestor
select
[Measures].[Internet Sales Amount]
on columns,
ancestor([Customer].[Customer Geography].[Customer].
[Crystal Zheng],[Customer].[Customer Geography].[City])
on rows
from
[Adventure Works]
-- alternative (2)Syntax
select
[Measures].[Internet Sales Amount]
on columns,
ancestor([Customer].[Customer Geography].[Customer].[Crystal Zheng],2)
on rows
from
[Adventure Works]
```

Result

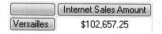

	Internet Sales Amount
Versailles	$102,657.25

Analysis

The first variation on the Ancestor syntax explicitly uses the City level (second parameter). The second variation asks to go two levels up (again, the second parameter). Either form of the syntax is easily adapted to navigate up to any level from any member of a hierarchy (the All level member does not have an ancestor).

Ascendants Function

The Ascendants function does rather more than the Ancestor function. Hopefully, this is one that is really worth trying. It's very popular in business intelligence (BI) reporting.

Syntax

```
-- ascendants
select
[Measures].[Internet Sales Amount]
on columns,
ascendants([Customer].[Customer Geography].[Customer].[Crystal Zheng])
on rows
from
[Adventure Works]
```

Result

	Internet Sales Amount
Crystal Zheng	$60.47
78000	$102,657.25
Versailles	$102,657.25
Yveline	$268,664.80
France	$2,644,017.71
All Customers	$29,358,677.22

Analysis

Some result for such a short query. It demonstrates the power, elegance, and simplicity of the MDX language. Given that we've tried quite a few navigation queries, the result is probably self-evident. As we saw earlier, the figure for the postal code is the same as the one for the city.

Ascendants with Hierarchize Function

Perhaps this one is even better. Our query introduces the Hierarchize function. Here it's used in conjunction with the Ascendants function.

Syntax

```
-- hierarchize
select
[Measures].[Internet Sales Amount]
on columns,
hierarchize(ascendants([Customer].[Customer Geography].
[Customer].[Crystal Zheng]))
on rows
from
[Adventure Works]
```

Result

	Internet Sales Amount
All Customers	$29,358,677.22
France	$2,644,017.71
Yveline	$268,664.80
Versailles	$102,657.25
78000	$102,657.25
Crystal Zheng	$60.47

Analysis

Hierarchize orders the members of the hierarchy from top to bottom. This is especially helpful for the set of members returned by Ascendants, but it can be used on any set of members of any hierarchy.

Combing Navigation Functions, Brothers and Sisters

The children of your parent are your brothers and sisters (siblings). Do we have any other customers with the same postal code (78000) as Crystal Zheng? The query includes .parent.children syntax.

Syntax

```
-- brothers and sisters in 78000 including Crystal
-- Zheng herself
select
[Measures].[Internet Sales Amount]
on columns,
[Customer].[Customer Geography].[Customer].[Crystal Zheng].parent.children
on rows
from
[Adventure Works]
```

Result

	Internet Sales Amount
Abby Sandberg	$5,948.23
Adam Hayes	$597.95
Alexa Peterson	$3,350.42
Blake Roberts	$8.99
Caleb Washington	$1,145.48
Carolyn Sanchez	$2,419.06
Chloe L. Ross	$2,049.10
Christian C. Davis	$7.28
Clayton C. Gao	$89.97
Colin M. Zheng	$38.98
Crystal Zheng	$60.47

Analysis

These are a few of the brothers and sisters of Crystal Zheng. The screenshot is a partial one. Interestingly, it includes Crystal Zheng herself, because she is a child of her parent. Elsewhere in the book the Except function is mentioned—you can easily adapt the query to exclude Crystal Zheng.

Siblings, Brothers and Sisters

A convenient shorthand for .parent.children is .siblings. This is another way of viewing the brothers and sisters of Crystal Zheng—all those customers with a postal code of 78000.

Syntax

```
-- brothers and sisters in 78000
select
[Measures].[Internet Sales Amount]
on columns,
[Customer].[Customer Geography].[Customer].[Crystal Zheng].siblings
on rows
from
[Adventure Works]
```

Result

	Internet Sales Amount
Abby Sandberg	$5,948.23
Adam Hayes	$597.95
Alexa Peterson	$3,350.42
Blake Roberts	$8.99
Caleb Washington	$1,145.48
Carolyn Sanchez	$2,419.06
Chloe L. Ross	$2,049.10
Christian C. Davis	$7.28
Clayton C. Gao	$89.97
Colin M. Zheng	$38.98
Crystal Zheng	$60.47

Analysis

Here we have a result identical to the previous query. Less intuitively, this time, Crystal Zheng is returned as a sibling of herself. Again, the Except function would be handy here (Except is covered elsewhere in the book). You could achieve the same result by querying the children of postal code 78000—the difference is your starting point. You can start from Crystal Zheng or from 78000.

First Customer with .firstchild

Suppose you wanted to establish the first customer who has the same postal code as Crystal Zheng. The query here introduces the .firstchild property function.

Syntax

```
-- first sibling in 78000
select
[Measures].[Internet Sales Amount]
on columns,
[Customer].[Customer Geography].[Customer].[Crystal Zheng].parent.firstchild
on rows
from
[Adventure Works]
```

Result

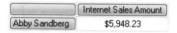

	Internet Sales Amount
Abby Sandberg	$5,948.23

Analysis

The first customer with the same postal code (78000) as Crystal Zheng is Abby Sandberg. As it stands, the concept of first customer is a little vague. The first customer is determined by the OrderBy property back in BIDS. Typically, but not always, members are ordered by either the attribute key or the attribute name. The latter gives an alphabetical sort, as is the case here.

First Customer with .firstsibling

A popular shorthand for .parent.firstchild is .firstsibling.

Syntax

```
-- first sibling in 78000
select
[Measures].[Internet Sales Amount]
on columns,
[Customer].[Customer Geography].[Customer].[Crystal Zheng].firstsibling
on rows
from
[Adventure Works]
```

Result

	Internet Sales Amount
Abby Sandberg	$5,948.23

Analysis

As you might have expected, this produces the same result.

Now for the Last Customer

Who's the last customer with the same postal district as Crystal Zheng? The property functions .parent.lastchild accomplish this.

Syntax

```
-- last sibling in 78000
select
[Measures].[Internet Sales Amount]
on columns,
[Customer].[Customer Geography].[Customer].[Crystal Zheng].parent
.lastchild
on rows
from
[Adventure Works]
```

Result

	Internet Sales Amount
Xavier White	$3.99

Analysis

Again, you need to be aware of the OrderBy property in your dimension design in BIDS. Often, such navigation functions make a lot of sense with dates (for example, what is the last day of the month of a particular date for which we have a member?).

The Last Customer Another Way

This query demonstrates the .lastsibling function, which is a shorthand for .parent .lastchild.

Syntax

```
-- last sibling 78000
select
[Measures].[Internet Sales Amount]
on columns,
[Customer].[Customer Geography].[Customer].[Crystal Zheng].lastsibling
on rows
from
[Adventure Works]
```

Result

	Internet Sales Amount
Xavier White	$3.99

Analysis

The result is identical to the last query. As is often the case, there is usually more than one way to retrieve the same cellset. The Tail function with a parameter of 1 would also give the same result. The Tail function is covered shortly.

Applying Vertical Navigation 1/2

Let's extend our application of some of the vertical navigation functions. How would you list all the customers in Yveline, if you already know the name of the state-province?

Syntax

```
-- fellow customers of Crystal Zheng in Yveline (her
-- state-province) 1/2
select
[Measures].[Internet Sales Amount]
on columns,
descendants([Customer].[Customer Geography].[State-Province].
[Yveline],[Customer].[Customer Geography].[Customer])
on rows
from
[Adventure Works]
```

Result

	Internet Sales Amount
Abby P. Rana	$36.96
Aidan Washington	$548.98
Alexa Morris	$553.97
Alison Sharma	$60.47
Anne Alonso	$597.95
Beth R. Alonso	$5,923.23
Billy L. Jiménez	$39.98
Bryan E. Bailey	$3,010.03
Charles J. Bell	$7.28
Charles M. Smith	$36.27

Analysis

This is a partial screenshot. This query is by way of revision; we looked at the Descendants function earlier. Shortly, we are going to extend our knowledge of Descendants.

Applying Vertical Navigation 2/2

How would you list all the customers in Yveline, if you don't know the name of the state-province and you want to see everyone with the same state-province as Crystal Zheng?

Syntax

```
-- fellow customers of Crystal Zheng in Yveline (her
-- state-province) 2/2
select
[Measures].[Internet Sales Amount]
on columns,
descendants(ancestor([Customer].[Customer Geography].
[Customer].[Crystal Zheng],[Customer].[Customer Geography].
[State-Province]),[Customer].[Customer Geography].[Customer])
on rows
from
[Adventure Works]
```

Result

	Internet Sales Amount
Abby P. Rana	$36.96
Aidan Washington	$548.98
Alexa Morris	$553.97
Alison Sharma	$60.47
Anne Alonso	$597.95
Beth R. Alonso	$5,923.23
Billy L. Jiménez	$39.98
Bryan E. Bailey	$3,010.03
Charles J. Bell	$7.28
Charles M. Smith	$36.27

Analysis

Many, many MDX queries utilize the navigation functions. With a little imagination, you are now in the position to begin applying them to your own cube(s).

Extending the Descendants Functionality

The Descendants function is incredibly versatile. Before we move on, here's a query we met earlier.

Syntax

```
-- all French cities
select
[Measures].[Internet Sales Amount]
on columns,
descendants([Customer].[Customer Geography].[Country].[France],[Customer]
.[Customer Geography].[City])
on rows
from
[Adventure Works]
```

Result

	Internet Sales Amount
Saint Ouen	$34,441.73
Les Ulis	$181,244.73
Morangis	$56,432.84
Verrieres Le Buisson	$41,619.61
Colomiers	$54,641.72
Aujan Mournede	(null)
Boulogne-Billancourt	$14,289.24
Colombes	$90,268.51
Courbevoie	$38,809.63
Paris La Defense	$45,350.86
Sèvres	$39,598.20

Analysis

Take some time to review the syntax. The Descendants function in this example has two parameters: first, the member (France) and, second, the level (City) at which you want to see the descendants of the member.

Descendants with self

A third parameter (self) is introduced into the Descendants function.

Syntax

```
-- all French cities - self
select
[Measures].[Internet Sales Amount]
on columns,
descendants([Customer].[Customer Geography].[Country]
.[France],[Customer].[Customer Geography].[City],self)
on rows
from
[Adventure Works]
```

Result

	Internet Sales Amount
Saint Ouen	$34,441.73
Les Ulis	$181,244.73
Morangis	$56,432.84
Verrieres Le Buisson	$41,619.61
Colomiers	$54,641.72
Aujan Mournede	(null)
Boulogne-Billancourt	$14,289.24
Colombes	$90,268.51
Courbevoie	$38,809.63
Paris La Defense	$45,350.86
Sèvres	$39,598.20

Analysis

Exactly the same result as before. The third parameter (self) is the default if you omit it altogether. It means "show the members of the specified level (City) stipulated."

Descendants with self_and_after

The third parameter (self) is now self_and_after.

Syntax

```
-- all cities and postal codes and customers
select
[Measures].[Internet Sales Amount]
on columns,
descendants([Customer].[Customer Geography].[Country].[France],
[Customer].[Customer Geography].[City],self_and_after)
on rows
from
[Adventure Works]
```

Result

	Internet Sales Amount
Saint Ouen	$34,441.73
17490	$34,441.73
Brad Nath	$48.97
Bridget C. Nath	$1,560.43
Chelsea Jordan	$1,735.98
Clayton Zhang	$2,049.10
Colin R. Wang	$47.97
Craig R. Gill	$23.78
Darren A. Ruiz	$43.46
Dominic A. Garcia	$1,382.97
Edwin Zhou	$2,753.82

Analysis

Self_and_after means "show the members of the level specified (City) and all the members of all those levels down to and including the leaf-level." Saint Ouen is a city in France. 17490 is a postal code in Saint Ouen. Brad Nath is a customer with a postal code of 17490. You will need to scroll to see all of the cities, postal codes, and customers. There are 1,894 rows, excluding the row for the column header Internet Sales Amount.

Descendants with after

Replace the third parameter (self_and_after) with after.

Syntax

```
-- just postal codes and customers - after
select
[Measures].[Internet Sales Amount]
on columns,
```

```
descendants([Customer].[Customer Geography].[Country]
.[France],[Customer].[Customer Geography].[City],after)
on rows
from
[Adventure Works]
```

Result

	Internet Sales Amount
17490	$34,441.73
Brad Nath	$48.97
Bridget C. Nath	$1,560.43
Chelsea Jordan	$1,735.98
Clayton Zhang	$2,049.10
Colin R. Wang	$47.97
Craig R. Gill	$23.78
Darren A. Ruiz	$43.46
Dominic A. Garcia	$1,382.97
Edwin Zhou	$2,753.82

Analysis

The cities, including Saint Ouen, have disappeared. The third parameter for the Descendants function is after rather than self_and_after. Self represents the second parameter (the City level). The parameter after represents everything below the City level in the hierarchy.

Descendants with before

In this variation of the Descendants query, the third parameter is before.

Syntax

```
-- just state-provinces and France itself -- before
select
[Measures].[Internet Sales Amount]
on columns,
descendants([Customer].[Customer Geography].[Country]
.[France],[Customer].[Customer Geography].[City],before)
on rows
from
[Adventure Works]
```

Result

	Internet Sales Amount
France	$2,644,017.71
Charente-Maritime	$34,441.73
Essonne	$279,297.18
Garonne (Haute)	$54,641.72
Gers	(null)
Hauts de Seine	$263,416.19
Loir et Cher	$21,473.74
Loiret	$91,562.91
Moselle	$94,046.23
Nord	$391,400.20
Pas de Calais	$11,342.92
Seine (Paris)	$539,725.80
Seine et Marne	$109,735.24
Seine Saint Denis	$379,479.75
Somme	$29,555.28
Val de Marne	$28,478.12
Val d'Oise	$46,755.90
Yveline	$268,664.80

Analysis

Here you can see everything that comes higher than the City level in the hierarchy, up to and including the starting member (France). We have rows showing the country France and all the state-provinces in France.

Descendants Using a Distance

This is the same as the last query except the City level has been replaced by the number 2.

Syntax

```
--using a distance - down to city with before
select
[Measures].[Internet Sales Amount]
on columns,
descendants([Customer].[Customer Geography].[Country].[France],2,before)
on rows
from
[Adventure Works]
```

Result

	Internet Sales Amount
France	$2,644,017.71
Charente-Maritime	$34,441.73
Essonne	$279,297.18
Garonne (Haute)	$54,641.72
Gers	(null)
Hauts de Seine	$263,416.19
Loir et Cher	$21,473.74
Loiret	$91,562.91
Moselle	$94,046.23
Nord	$391,400.20
Pas de Calais	$11,342.92
Seine (Paris)	$539,725.80
Seine et Marne	$109,735.24
Seine Saint Denis	$379,479.75
Somme	$29,555.28
Val de Marne	$28,478.12
Val d'Oise	$46,755.90
Yveline	$268,664.80

Analysis

Go down two levels (that is, to the City level) and show everything higher in the hierarchy, up to and including the starting member (France).

Cousin

Most of the navigation queries so far (apart from siblings) involve vertical navigation up and down hierarchies. Often you want to navigate horizontally. Cousin is just such a function.

Syntax

```
-- using cousin - horizontal navigation
select
{[Date].[Calendar].[Calendar Quarter].[Q1 CY 2003],cousin([Date]
.[Calendar].[Calendar Quarter].[Q1 CY 2003],[Date].[Calendar].
[Calendar Year].[CY 2004])}
on columns,
[Measures].[Reseller Sales Amount]
```

```
on rows
from
[Adventure Works]
```

Result

	Q1 CY 2003	Q1 CY 2004
Reseller Sales Amount	$5,266,343.51	$7,102,685.11

Analysis

The first member on the Columns axis is Q1 CY 2003. The second member is Q1 CY 2004, exactly a year after. Cousin expects two parameters. The first parameter (Q1 CY 2003) is the starting member. The second parameter (CY 2004) is a member at a higher level in the hierarchy. The result is to return the member that is a descendant of that higher level at the same level and in the same relative position (relative to its own ancestor at the higher level) as the starting member. Would you like that in English? CY 2004 (second parameter) is a member of the Calendar Year level. Q1 CY 2003 (first parameter) is part of the calendar year CY 2003. Q1 CY 2003 is a member of the Calendar Quarter level. Q1 CY 2003 is the first quarter of CY 2003. The first quarter of CY 2004 is Q1 CY 2004. Therefore, it returns Q1 CY 2004! I guess you have to try Cousin a few times before it becomes obvious.

More on Cousin

Cousin is one of the least intuitive MDX functions. Of course, it's also one of the most useful. Here's a more difficult example to test your understanding.

Syntax

```
-- less obvious cousin
select
{ [Date].[Calendar].[Calendar Quarter].[Q1 CY 2003],
cousin([Date].[Calendar].[Calendar Quarter].[Q1 CY 2003],
[Date].[Calendar].[Calendar Semester].[H2 CY 2003])}
on columns,
[Measures].[Reseller Sales Amount]
on rows
from
[Adventure Works]
```

Result

	Q1 CY 2003	Q3 CY 2003
Reseller Sales Amount	$5,266,343.51	$10,926,196.09

Analysis

Here, the higher level is Calendar Semester (half-year). Q1 CY 2003 (first parameter) is the first quarter of its own semester. The first quarter of the second semester (HY2 CY 2003) is Q3 CY 2003. Q3 CY 2003 is the member returned. Cousin is handy when you need to establish a range for MDX calculations. There is more on this elsewhere in the book.

A Simple Range

Horizontal navigation is often used to establish the end point (or start point) of a range of members. Ranges play a big part in BI reports.

Syntax

```
-- a simple range
select
{[Date].[Calendar].[Calendar Quarter].[Q1 CY 2003],
[Date].[Calendar].[Calendar Quarter].[Q2 CY 2003],
[Date].[Calendar].[Calendar Quarter].[Q3 CY 2003]}
on columns,
[Measures].[Reseller Sales Amount]
on rows
from
[Adventure Works]
```

Result

	Q1 CY 2003	Q2 CY 2003	Q3 CY 2003
Reseller Sales Amount	$5,266,343.51	$6,733,903.82	$10,926,196.09

Analysis

This is a range of members across three quarters. It has a start point (Q1) and an end point (Q3). There is also an intermediate point (Q2).

A Simpler Simple Range

Q2 CY 2003 is no longer explicitly mentioned. It has been replaced with the colon range operator (:).

Syntax

```
-- a simple range with colon operator
select
[Date].[Calendar].[Calendar Quarter].[Q1 CY 2003]:
[Date].[Calendar].[Calendar Quarter].[Q3 CY 2003]
on columns,
[Measures].[Reseller Sales Amount]
on rows
from
[Adventure Works]
```

Result

	Q1 CY 2003	Q2 CY 2003	Q3 CY 2003
Reseller Sales Amount	$5,266,343.51	$6,733,903.82	$10,926,196.09

Analysis

There are a few things to mention. One, you don't need the braces ({ }) delimiters when you use the colon (:) range operator. Two, the colon operator (:) means you only have to type or drag the start point and end point and not the intermediate point. You might have many intermediate members, so this method saves a lot of work.

Range with Cousin

Only the start point is explicit. Neither the end point nor the intermediate point is hard-coded. The Cousin function and the colon operator (:) are used instead.

Syntax

```
-- range with cousin
select
[Date].[Calendar].[Calendar Quarter].[Q1 CY 2003]:cousin([Date]
.[Calendar].[Calendar Quarter].[Q1 CY 2003],[Date].[Calendar].
[Calendar Semester].[H2 CY 2003])
on columns,
```

```
[Measures].[Reseller Sales Amount]
on rows
from
[Adventure Works]
```

Result

	Q1 CY 2003	Q2 CY 2003	Q3 CY 2003
Reseller Sales Amount	$5,266,343.51	$6,733,903.82	$10,926,196.09

Analysis

This is a really useful query. You don't need to know anything about member names (or keys) apart from the name (or key) of the member at the start point of the range. By transposing the expressions on either side of the colon (:), you only need to know the end point of the range.

Positive Lead and Negative Lag

Lead (with a positive number) means "jump ahead horizontally at the same level." Lag (with a positive number) means "jump back."

Syntax

```
-- lead positive second
select
{[Date].[Calendar].[Calendar Quarter].[Q1 CY 2003],
[Date].[Calendar].[Calendar Quarter].[Q1 CY 2003].lead(2)}
on columns,
[Measures].[Reseller Sales Amount]
on rows
from
[Adventure Works]
-- lag negative second
select
{[Date].[Calendar].[Calendar Quarter].[Q1 CY 2003],
[Date].[Calendar].[Calendar Quarter].[Q1 CY 2003].lag(-2)}
on columns,
[Measures].[Reseller Sales Amount]
on rows
from
[Adventure Works]
```

Result

	Q1 CY 2003	Q3 CY 2003
Reseller Sales Amount	$5,266,343.51	$10,926,196.09

Analysis

Lead(2) jumps two quarters into the future. Lag(-2) also means jump ahead by two quarters. Both queries return the same result.

Negative Lead and Positive Lag

Here's some more on the lead and lag property functions. We have made a few subtle changes from the previous two queries.

Syntax

```
-- lead negative first
select
{[Date].[Calendar].[Calendar Quarter].[Q3 CY 2003].
lead(-2),[Date].[Calendar].[Calendar Quarter].[Q3 CY 2003]}
on columns,
[Measures].[Reseller Sales Amount]
on rows
from
[Adventure Works]
-- lag positive first
select
{[Date].[Calendar].[Calendar Quarter].[Q3 CY 2003].
lag(2),[Date].[Calendar].[Calendar Quarter].[Q3 CY 2003]}
on columns,
[Measures].[Reseller Sales Amount]
on rows
from
[Adventure Works]
```

Result

	Q1 CY 2003	Q3 CY 2003
Reseller Sales Amount	$5,266,343.51	$10,926,196.09

Analysis

Lead(-2), go two quarters back. Lag(2), the same. Again, both queries have the same result. In fact, the result is the same as the previous two queries as well. Your results are determined by whether you use lead or lag, whether you use positive or negative numbers as the function parameter, and where in the set you position the member with the lead or lag function.

Lead (or Lag) with a Range

Here you witness one of the main reasons for using lead (or lag). It's handy for setting up ranges.

Syntax

```
-- lead (or lag) with a range
select
[Date].[Calendar].[Calendar Quarter].[Q1 CY 2003]
:[Date].[Calendar].[Calendar Quarter].[Q1 CY 2003].lead(2)
on columns,
[Measures].[Reseller Sales Amount]
on rows
from
[Adventure Works]
```

Result

	Q1 CY 2003	Q2 CY 2003	Q3 CY 2003
Reseller Sales Amount	$5,266,343.51	$6,733,903.82	$10,926,196.09

Analysis

Of course, lag(-2) would have accomplished the same. Lead and lag are much simpler than Cousin. However, lead and lag require that you know how far to jump. Cousin, on the other hand, does not—it finds the start or end point for you by relative position. Lead and lag may let you down when members (especially in a time dimension) are not both consecutive and contiguous. This is one of the arguments for using a server time dimension rather than a hand-rolled time dimension in the source star schema. A server time dimension is a part of your dimension design in BIDS. A server time dimension ensures that dates are consecutive and contiguous. In practice, however, server time dimensions are not used very much—they have one or two other disadvantages. Perhaps the best approach is to create a time dimension without any "gaps," maybe using an SQL

While loop with start and end dates. If you base your time dimension on existing dates in your transactional relational database system, you may end up with "gaps."

Head

Head is not a navigation function. Rather it is one of the set functions. You can verify this by viewing the Functions pane. The Functions tab is next to the Metadata tab. However, the results are similar to those produced by the navigation functions, so it's included here for completeness.

Syntax

```
--head
select
{[Measures].[Internet Sales Amount],[Measures].[Internet Tax Amount]}
on columns,
head([Customer].[Customer Geography].[Country],2)
on rows
from
[Adventure Works]
```

Result

	Internet Sales Amount	Internet Tax Amount
Australia	$9,061,000.58	$724,880.07
Canada	$1,977,844.86	$158,227.59

Analysis

The first parameter for Head is a set (here, the members of the Country level). The second parameter is a number (here it is 2). Show me the first two members of the Country level.

Tail

Show me the last three members of the Country level.

Syntax

```
--tail
select
{[Measures].[Internet Sales Amount],[Measures].[Internet Tax Amount]}
on columns,
```

```
tail([Customer].[Customer Geography].[Country],3)
on rows
from
[Adventure Works]
```

Result

	Internet Sales Amount	Internet Tax Amount
Germany	$2,894,312.34	$231,544.99
United Kingdom	$3,391,712.21	$271,336.98
United States	$9,389,789.51	$751,183.18

Analysis

If you omit the second numeric parameter, it defaults to 1. This will find the last member of a set. You may want to exploit this to determine the end point for a range.

prevmember

Here's a query showing Germany and the result of the .prevmember function on Germany. Functionally, prevmember is the same as lag(1).

Syntax

```
-- prevmember
select
{[Measures].[Internet Sales Amount],[Measures].[Internet Tax Amount]}
on columns,
{[Customer].[Customer Geography].[Country].[Germany],
[Customer].[Customer Geography].[Country].[Germany].prevmember}
on rows
from
[Adventure Works]
-- lag equivalent
select
{[Measures].[Internet Sales Amount],[Measures].[Internet Tax Amount]}
on columns,
{[Customer].[Customer Geography].[Country].[Germany],
[Customer].[Customer Geography].[Country].[Germany].lag(1)}
on rows
from
[Adventure Works]
```

Result

	Internet Sales Amount	Internet Tax Amount
Germany	$2,894,312.34	$231,544.99
France	$2,644,017.71	$211,521.42

Analysis

Both queries have identical outcomes. Often, prevmember will prove more useful in time dimensions. Germany and France positions are probably arbitrary and based solely on an alphabetic sort.

prevmember.prevmember

This query shows how to jump back two places.

Syntax

```
-- prevmember.prevmember
select
{[Measures].[Internet Sales Amount],[Measures].[Internet Tax Amount]}
on columns,
{[Customer].[Customer Geography].[Country].[Germany],
[Customer].[Customer Geography].[Country].[Germany].prevmember.prevmember}
on rows
from
[Adventure Works]
```

Result

	Internet Sales Amount	Internet Tax Amount
Germany	$2,894,312.34	$231,544.99
Canada	$1,977,844.86	$158,227.59

Analysis

This query selects Germany, then jumps two back to Canada and skips France. This is more useful when the alphabetic (or key) position of a member has meaning to you.

nextmember

This query demonstrates how to jump ahead by one.

Syntax

```
-- nextmember
select
{[Measures].[Internet Sales Amount],[Measures].[Internet Tax Amount]}
on columns,
{[Customer].[Customer Geography].[Country].[Germany],
[Customer].[Customer Geography].[Country].[Germany].nextmember}
on rows
from
[Adventure Works]
```

Result

	Internet Sales Amount	Internet Tax Amount
Germany	$2,894,312.34	$231,544.99
United Kingdom	$3,391,712.21	$271,336.98

Analysis

Here, we are reversing the direction of our horizontal navigation.

nextmember.nextmember

This query demonstrates jumping ahead by two.

Syntax

```
-- nextmember.nextmember
select
{[Measures].[Internet Sales Amount],[Measures].[Internet Tax Amount]}
on columns,
{[Customer].[Customer Geography].[Country].[Germany],
[Customer].[Customer Geography].[Country].[Germany].nextmember.nextmember}
on rows
from
[Adventure Works]
```

Result

	Internet Sales Amount	Internet Tax Amount
Germany	$2,894,312.34	$231,544.99
United States	$9,389,789.51	$751,183.18

Analysis
MDX is straightforward!

nextmember with a Range
This time, yet another navigation query—or rather, two queries. Functionally, they are equivalent.

Syntax

```
-- range with nextmember
select
{[Measures].[Internet Sales Amount],[Measures].[Internet Tax Amount]}
on columns,
[Customer].[Customer Geography].[Country].[Germany]
:[Customer].[Customer Geography].[Country].[Germany].nextmember.nextmember
on rows
from
[Adventure Works]
-- lead equivalent
select
{[Measures].[Internet Sales Amount],[Measures].[Internet Tax Amount]}
on columns,
[Customer].[Customer Geography].[Country].[Germany]
:[Customer].[Customer Geography].[Country].[Germany].lead(2)
on rows
from
[Adventure Works]
```

Result

	Internet Sales Amount	Internet Tax Amount
Germany	$2,894,312.34	$231,544.99
United Kingdom	$3,391,712.21	$271,336.98
United States	$9,389,789.51	$751,183.18

Analysis
Now you should have a few ideas of how to navigate your cube(s). MDX (unlike SQL) is positionally aware.

Descendants with an Unbalanced Hierarchy 1/2

You may or may not meet unbalanced hierarchies as you work with your own cubes. The Employee dimension in Adventure Works contains an unbalanced hierarchy called Employees. This is based on a source star schema dimension table that's a parent-child (self-join) table. Unbalanced hierarchies need special attention.

Syntax

```
-- descendants unbalanced hierarchy 1/2 - 28 rows
select
{}
on columns,
descendants([Employee].[Employees].[Ken J. Sánchez],
[Employee].[Employees].[Employee Level 06])
on rows
from
[Adventure Works]
```

Result

Jo L. Berry
Lori K. Penor
Pat H. Coleman
Stuart J. Macrae
Annette L. Hill
Arvind B. Rao
Ben T. Miller
Eric S. Kurjan
Erin M. Hagens
Frank S. Pellow
Fukiko J. Ogisu

Analysis

The result set shown is partial. You may need to scroll down to see all the rows. There are 28 rows—you can verify this easily by clicking the Messages tab. This indicates that 28 employees at level 06 report directly (or indirectly) to Ken J. Sánchez. It's important to note the accented character in Sánchez. You can use Windows Character Map (charmap.exe) to type or paste this if it's not directly supported on your keyboard. Alternatively, you could replace the name [Ken J. Sánchez] with the key &[112].

Descendants with an Unbalanced Hierarchy 2/2

This is our final navigation query. It's an alternative to the last query and gives different results. You probably need to consider both versions when you work on your own unbalanced hierarchies.

Syntax

```
-- descendants unbalanced hierarchy 2/2 - 249 rows
select
{}
on columns,
descendants([Employee].[Employees].[Ken J. Sánchez],,leaves)
on rows
from
[Adventure Works]
```

Result

Jae B. Pak
Rachel B. Valdez
Ranjit R. Varkey Chudukatil
David R. Campbell
Garrett R. Vargas
Jillian Carson
José Edvaldo. Saraiva
Linda C. Mitchell
Michael G. Blythe
Pamela O. Ansman-Wolfe
Shu K. Ito

Analysis

Again, this is only a partial result set. If you click the Messages tab you should see that there are 249 rows this time—rather more than in the previous query. Both answers are correct! The syntax here shows that there is no level as the second parameter to Descendants and that the third parameter is Leaves. In effect, it returns all employees (no matter which level) that are at the bottom of the hierarchy. For example, Jae B. Pak reports indirectly to Ken J. Sánchez but is at level 05, and he has no one at level 06 reporting to him. The employees listed might include some at level 03, level 04, and level 05 and will include all those at level 06 (the lowest level). Our last query simply returned all the ones at level 06 and no others.

Chapter 4

Bringing Order: Sorting Results

This chapter introduces various ways of sorting the results of your queries. Business intelligence reports often have a requirement to put information in some kind of order—whether numeric or alphabetic. This chapter shows you just how to do this.

▶   **Key concepts**   Ordering by attribute, ordering by measure inside and outside hierarchies

▶   **Keywords**   Order, Asc, BAsc, Desc, BDesc, Hierarchize, Post

By Default, Measures Are Not Sorted

There are two types of sorting. Attributes are often sorted alphabetically (or sometimes by a key or some other attribute). The second type of sort is sorting on measures. This is not part of the measure design in BIDS but is exclusively your responsibility as your company's MDX guru. By default, measures are not sorted, as this query demonstrates.

Syntax

```
-- unsorted on Internet Sales Amount
select
[Measures].[Internet Sales Amount]
on columns,
[Product].[Product Categories].[Subcategory]
on rows
from
[Adventure Works]
```

Result

	Internet Sales Amount
Bike Racks	$39,360.00
Bike Stands	$39,591.00
Bottles and Cages	$56,798.19
Cleaners	$7,218.60
Fenders	$46,619.58
Helmets	$225,335.60
Hydration Packs	$40,307.67
Lights	(null)
Locks	(null)
Panniers	(null)
Pumps	(null)
Tires and Tubes	$245,529.32
Mountain Bikes	$9,952,759.56

Analysis

There is no apparent sorting of the Internet Sales Amount measure. The first three rows for sales are in order, but that is purely a consequence of the subcategory attribute alphabetical sorting in BIDS. As you move down the rows, the figures follow no particular pattern. Incidentally (but beyond the scope of this book), the subcategories do seem to be sorted alphabetically. However, this breaks down somewhere around Tires and Tubes and Mountain Bikes. If you were to peek at the Product dimension design in BIDS, you would notice that subcategory has an OrderBy property of Name. This gives the alphabetical sort of the rows. However, our query requests subcategories as part of the Product Categories hierarchy—the subcategories are sorted on a per-category basis. Thus, Tires and Tubes is the last subcategory of its category (Accessories, which is not shown), and Mountain Bikes is the first subcategory in the Bikes category. To pursue the analysis, the subcategories for Accessories appear before those of Bikes because the category itself also has its OrderBy property set to Name.

Using Order

To sort your rows (or columns), you employ the Order function.

Syntax

```
-- order is ascending
select
[Measures].[Internet Sales Amount]
on columns,
order([Product].[Subcategory].[Subcategory],[Measures].
[Internet Sales Amount])
on rows
from
[Adventure Works]
```

Result

	Internet Sales Amount
Wheels	(null)
Socks	$5,106.32
Cleaners	$7,218.60
Caps	$19,688.10
Gloves	$35,020.70
Vests	$35,687.00
Bike Racks	$39,360.00
Bike Stands	$39,591.00
Hydration Packs	$40,307.67
Fenders	$46,619.58
Bottles and Cages	$56,798.19
Shorts	$71,319.81
Jerseys	$172,950.68
Helmets	$225,335.60
Tires and Tubes	$245,529.32
Touring Bikes	$3,844,801.05
Mountain Bikes	$9,952,759.56
Road Bikes	$14,520,584.04

Analysis

The first parameter is the set of rows to sort, and the second parameter is the measure to sort by. The result shows the subcategories sorted by Internet Sales Amount. You may have to scroll down to get beyond all the empty cells. The sort order is ascending, which is the default. Note that this query uses an attribute hierarchy ([Subcategory]. [Subcategory]) and not a user hierarchy.

Explicit Ascend

This query returns exactly the same result as the previous query.

Syntax

```
-- explicit ascend
select
[Measures].[Internet Sales Amount]
on columns,
order([Product].[Subcategory].[Subcategory],
[Measures].[Internet Sales Amount],asc)
on rows
from
[Adventure Works]
```

Result

	Internet Sales Amount
Wheels	(null)
Socks	$5,106.32
Cleaners	$7,218.60
Caps	$19,688.10
Gloves	$35,020.70
Vests	$35,687.00
Bike Racks	$39,360.00
Bike Stands	$39,591.00
Hydration Packs	$40,307.67
Fenders	$46,619.58
Bottles and Cages	$56,798.19
Shorts	$71,319.81
Jerseys	$172,950.68
Helmets	$225,335.60
Tires and Tubes	$245,529.32
Touring Bikes	$3,844,801.05
Mountain Bikes	$9,952,759.56
Road Bikes	$14,520,584.04

Analysis

All we did here was to add Asc as an additional parameter to the Order function. Maybe it's good practice to explicitly define the sort order.

Descending Sort

Simply by adding Desc, you can have a descending sort on sales.

Syntax

```
-- descending
select
[Measures].[Internet Sales Amount]
on columns,
order([Product].[Subcategory].[Subcategory],
[Measures].[Internet Sales Amount],desc)
on rows
from
[Adventure Works]
```

Result

	Internet Sales Amount
Road Bikes	$14,520,584.04
Mountain Bikes	$9,952,759.56
Touring Bikes	$3,844,801.05
Tires and Tubes	$245,529.32
Helmets	$225,335.60
Jerseys	$172,950.68
Shorts	$71,319.81
Bottles and Cages	$56,798.19
Fenders	$46,619.58
Hydration Packs	$40,307.67
Bike Stands	$39,591.00
Bike Racks	$39,360.00
Vests	$35,687.00
Gloves	$35,020.70
Caps	$19,688.10
Cleaners	$7,218.60
Socks	$5,106.32
Bib-Shorts	(null)

Analysis

This is quite handy when you want to see the highest sales at the top.

The Sort Only Works for a Few Rows

Here we ask for an explicit ascending sort on Internet Sales Amount.

Syntax

```
-- order seems to be ascending
select
[Measures].[Internet Sales Amount]
on columns,
order([Product].[Product Categories].[Subcategory],
[Measures].[Internet Sales Amount],asc)
on rows
from
[Adventure Works]
```

Result

	Internet Sales Amount
Caps	$19,688.10
Gloves	$35,020.70
Vests	$35,687.00
Shorts	$71,319.81
Jerseys	$172,950.68
Lights	(null)
Locks	(null)
Panniers	(null)
Pumps	(null)
Cleaners	$7,218.60
Bike Racks	$39,360.00

Analysis

As you scroll down the rows, all appears well until you get somewhere around Jerseys. Jerseys is followed by a few nulls, then Cleaners, which is a lower, not a higher, sales figure. A couple of queries ago, the ascending sort was working fine. Now it suddenly stops working. There is a subtle difference in the set specified for the Rows axis. This time I have used a user hierarchy ([Product Categories].[Subcategory]) rather than an attribute hierarchy ([Subcategory].[Subcategory]). The sort is respecting the structure of the user hierarchy. Try the next query and this will make more sense.

Breaking Hierarchies

Here's a very minor but important change. Asc has been replaced by Basc.

Syntax

```
-- basc might be better
select
[Measures].[Internet Sales Amount]
on columns,
order([Product].[Product Categories].[Subcategory],
[Measures].[Internet Sales Amount],basc)
on rows
from
[Adventure Works]
```

Result

	Internet Sales Amount
Wheels	(null)
Socks	$5,106.32
Cleaners	$7,218.60
Caps	$19,688.10
Gloves	$35,020.70
Vests	$35,687.00
Bike Racks	$39,360.00
Bike Stands	$39,591.00
Hydration Packs	$40,307.67
Fenders	$46,619.58
Bottles and Cages	$56,798.19
Shorts	$71,319.81
Jerseys	$172,950.68
Helmets	$225,335.60
Tires and Tubes	$245,529.32
Touring Bikes	$3,844,801.05
Mountain Bikes	$9,952,759.56
Road Bikes	$14,520,584.04

Analysis

You might have to scroll a little to get beyond the empty cells. This query and the previous one show two ways of sorting with the Order function. If you have a user hierarchy rather than an attribute hierarchy, you have a choice of the sort observing the hierarchy or ignoring (breaking) the hierarchy. The letter *B* in front of Asc means "break the hierarchy." If you want, return to the result of the previous query. There, the sort has worked—only the sort of the subcategories restarts as the category (not shown) changes. The category level is the next level up from the subcategory level in the Product Categories user hierarchy. If you desire, you could also show the category name as well as the subcategory name. You can accomplish this by writing a crossjoin query on the [Category] and the [Subcategory] attribute hierarchies—more on that topic elsewhere. Both breaking and nonbreaking sorts are valid. Your choice is a business decision. A crossjoin sort example appears at the end of this chapter.

Order with desc on User Hierarchy

Let's reverse the sort order to see the effect of user hierarchies on a descending sort.

Syntax

```
-- desc
select
```

```
[Measures].[Internet Sales Amount]
on columns,
order([Product].[Product Categories].[Subcategory],
[Measures].[Internet Sales Amount],desc)
on rows
from
[Adventure Works]
```

Result

	Internet Sales Amount
Bike Racks	$39,360.00
Cleaners	$7,218.60
Lights	(null)
Locks	(null)
Panniers	(null)
Pumps	(null)
Jerseys	$172,950.68

Analysis

If you move down to somewhere around Bike Racks, you can witness the descending sort restarting for the Jerseys subcategory as the parent category (hidden) changes.

Order with bdesc on User Hierarchy

Now it's time to break the hierarchy and compare the output with that of the last query.

Syntax

```
-- bdesc
select
[Measures].[Internet Sales Amount]
on columns,
order([Product].[Product Categories].[Subcategory],
[Measures].[Internet Sales Amount],bdesc)
on rows
from
[Adventure Works]
```

Result

	Internet Sales Amount
Road Bikes	$14,520,584.04
Mountain Bikes	$9,952,759.56
Touring Bikes	$3,844,801.05
Tires and Tubes	$245,529.32
Helmets	$225,335.60
Jerseys	$172,950.68
Shorts	$71,319.81
Bottles and Cages	$56,798.19
Fenders	$46,619.58
Hydration Packs	$40,307.67
Bike Stands	$39,591.00
Bike Racks	$39,360.00
Vests	$35,687.00
Gloves	$35,020.70
Caps	$19,688.10
Cleaners	$7,218.60
Socks	$5,106.32
Lights	(null)

Analysis

When you break the hierarchy, it looks like an SQL sort with an Order By clause. Sometimes this is what you want, but often end users want sorting within groups. Then you won't want to break the hierarchy.

Sorting a Measure by Another Hidden Measure

An interesting business problem—how to show the Internet Sales Amount for subcategories, but sorted by the Reseller Sales Amount.

Syntax

```
-- sorting by another column from the one displayed
select
[Measures].[Internet Sales Amount]
on columns,
order([Product].[Product Categories].[Subcategory],
[Measures].[Reseller Sales Amount],bdesc)
on rows
from
[Adventure Works]
```

Result

	Internet Sales Amount
Road Bikes	$14,520,584.04
Mountain Bikes	$9,952,759.56
Touring Bikes	$3,844,801.05
Mountain Frames	(null)
Road Frames	(null)
Touring Frames	(null)
Wheels	(null)
Jerseys	$172,950.68
Shorts	$71,319.81
Helmets	$225,335.60
Vests	$35,687.00
Gloves	$35,020.70

Analysis

The second parameter of the Order function has been changed from Internet Sales Amount to Reseller Sales Amount. The measure in the display (Internet Sales Amount) is neither sorted by breaking the hierarchy nor by nonbreaking of the hierarchy. The former can be ruled out by noting that the value for Helmets is larger than that for Shorts. The latter can be ruled out because Helmets (in the Accessories category) lies between Shorts and Vests (both in the Clothing category). It's sometimes really helpful to have a pivot table on the cube open as you write your MDX—it lets you drill down and up easily so you can help verify your MDX query results. That's how I did a quick check to see whether Helmets was in Clothing. Your query editor Metadata pane does not support the drill down or drill up of user hierarchies.

Showing the Hidden Sort Measure

To be absolutely certain that the last query did indeed work, add another measure to the Columns axis.

Syntax

```
-- proof
select
{[Measures].[Internet Sales Amount],[Measures].[Reseller Sales Amount]}
on columns,
order([Product].[Product Categories].[Subcategory],
[Measures].[Reseller Sales Amount],bdesc)
on rows
from
[Adventure Works]
```

Result

	Internet Sales Amount	Reseller Sales Amount
Road Bikes	$14,520,584.04	$29,358,206.96
Mountain Bikes	$9,952,759.56	$26,492,684.38
Touring Bikes	$3,844,801.05	$10,451,490.22
Mountain Frames	(null)	$4,713,672.15
Road Frames	(null)	$3,849,853.34
Touring Frames	(null)	$1,642,327.69
Wheels	(null)	$679,070.07
Jerseys	$172,950.68	$579,308.71
Shorts	$71,319.81	$342,202.72
Helmets	$225,335.60	$258,712.93
Vests	$35,687.00	$223,801.37

Analysis

Hopefully, this demonstrates why Shorts came before Helmets and why Helmets appeared between Shorts and Vests.

Sorting Columns Rather Than Rows

There is nothing at all to prevent you from sorting across columns instead of down rows.

Syntax

```
-- sort across columns as well as down rows
select
order([Product].[Product Categories].[Subcategory],
[Measures].[Reseller Sales Amount],bdesc)
on columns,
{[Measures].[Internet Sales Amount],[Measures].[Reseller Sales Amount]}
on rows
from
[Adventure Works]
```

Result

	Road Bikes	Mountain Bikes	Touring Bikes	Mountain Frames	Road Frames	Touring Frames	Wheels	Jerseys	Shorts
Internet Sales Amount	$14,520,584.04	$9,952,759.56	$3,844,801.05	(null)	(null)	(null)	(null)	$172,950.68	$71,319.81
Reseller Sales Amount	$29,358,206.96	$26,492,684.38	$10,451,490.22	$4,713,672.15	$3,849,853.34	$1,642,327.69	$679,070.07	$579,308.71	$342,202.72

Analysis

Except the fact it may be more difficult to read.

Sorting Hierarchies, Not Measures

I've been a little lazy in my MDX, not really paying attention to the order of the members in the set on the Rows axis.

Syntax

```
-- some haphazard rows
select
[Measures].[Internet Sales Amount]
on columns,
{[Product].[Subcategory].[Touring Bikes],[Product].[Subcategory],[Product]
.[Subcategory].[Mountain Bikes]}
on rows
from
[Adventure Works]
```

Result

	Internet Sales Amount
Touring Bikes	$3,844,801.05
All Products	$29,358,677.22
Mountain Bikes	$9,952,759.56

Analysis

This is an attribute hierarchy. If you check the Metadata pane, it's a blue rectangle, not a pyramid. I also cut corners in my typing: [Product].[Subcategory].[Subcategory] is better than [Product].[Subcategory] because the double repeated name for the hierarchy and the level lets you see at a glance that it's probably an attribute hierarchy rather than a user hierarchy. But the order of the rows still disturbs me!

Hierarchize Function

This is the same query but with the addition of the Hierarchize function.

Syntax

```
-- put into order of hierarchy
select
[Measures].[Internet Sales Amount]
on columns,
```

```
hierarchize({[Product].[Subcategory].[Touring Bikes],
[Product].[Subcategory],[Product].[Subcategory].[Mountain Bikes]})
on rows
from
[Adventure Works]
```

Result

	Internet Sales Amount
All Products	$29,358,677.22
Mountain Bikes	$9,952,759.56
Touring Bikes	$3,844,801.05

Analysis

Now I'm happier. Using Hierarchize is a nice way to tidy up. It doesn't imply a sort on cell values, even though it might look that way. It sorts from the top level of the hierarchy down. If there are more than two members on a particular level, it sorts according to the OrderBy property for the attribute at that level in BIDS.

Hierarchize Function, Upside Down

All that's happened here is the addition of the Post parameter.

Syntax

```
-- reverse order of hierarchy
select
[Measures].[Internet Sales Amount]
on columns,
hierarchize({[Product].[Subcategory].[Touring Bikes],
[Product].[Subcategory],[Product].[Subcategory].[Mountain Bikes]},post)
on rows
from
[Adventure Works]
```

Result

	Internet Sales Amount
Mountain Bikes	$9,952,759.56
Touring Bikes	$3,844,801.05
All Products	$29,358,677.22

Analysis

The addition of Post has caused the hierarchy to appear upside down. The result you can see should confirm that the sort has nothing to do with the measure in the cell values.

Real-World Example of Sorting 1/2

To learn MDX, it's probably best to do so one function, technique, or concept at a time. But we want real-world BI reports as soon as possible! So here's quite a nice query using the Order function. If you dipped into the book to read this chapter on sorting first, don't worry. Non Empty and Crossjoin are covered in detail elsewhere. By the time you reach the end of the book (if you persevere), you will be writing queries like this (and even more complex ones) within a second or two.

Syntax

```
-- crossjoin sorting example, non-breaking
select
[Measures].[Internet Sales Amount]
on columns,
non empty order(crossjoin([Product].[Category].[Category],
[Product].[Subcategory].[Subcategory]),
[Measures].[Internet Sales Amount],desc)
on rows
from
[Adventure Works]
```

Result

		Internet Sales Amount
Accessories	Tires and Tubes	$245,529.32
Accessories	Helmets	$225,335.60
Accessories	Bottles and Cages	$56,798.19
Accessories	Fenders	$46,619.58
Accessories	Hydration Packs	$40,307.67
Accessories	Bike Stands	$39,591.00
Accessories	Bike Racks	$39,360.00
Accessories	Cleaners	$7,218.60
Bikes	Road Bikes	$14,520,584.04
Bikes	Mountain Bikes	$9,952,759.56
Bikes	Touring Bikes	$3,844,801.05
Clothing	Jerseys	$172,950.68
Clothing	Shorts	$71,319.81
Clothing	Vests	$35,687.00
Clothing	Gloves	$35,020.70
Clothing	Caps	$19,688.10
Clothing	Socks	$5,106.32

Analysis

I guess, for once, you should just observe and not analyze. Simply enjoy the results of your skills. Oh, but wait, we really want Road Bikes at the top.

Real-World Example of Sorting 2/2

Road Bikes at the top. All we did was change Desc to Bdesc.

Syntax

```
-- crossjoin sorting example, breaking
select
[Measures].[Internet Sales Amount]
on columns,
non empty order(crossjoin([Product].[Category].[Category],
[Product].[Subcategory].[Subcategory]),
[Measures].[Internet Sales Amount],bdesc)
on rows
from
[Adventure Works]
```

Result

		Internet Sales Amount
Bikes	Road Bikes	$14,520,584.04
Bikes	Mountain Bikes	$9,952,759.56
Bikes	Touring Bikes	$3,844,801.05
Accessories	Tires and Tubes	$245,529.32
Accessories	Helmets	$225,335.60
Clothing	Jerseys	$172,950.68
Clothing	Shorts	$71,319.81
Accessories	Bottles and Cages	$56,798.19
Accessories	Fenders	$46,619.58
Accessories	Hydration Packs	$40,307.67
Accessories	Bike Stands	$39,591.00
Accessories	Bike Racks	$39,360.00
Clothing	Vests	$35,687.00
Clothing	Gloves	$35,020.70
Clothing	Caps	$19,688.10
Accessories	Cleaners	$7,218.60
Clothing	Socks	$5,106.32

Analysis

That's it. This is the last query in this chapter dedicated to sorting.

Chapter 5

Slice, Dice, and Filter: Using Where and Filter

O ften, you will want only a subset of your dimension members and measure values. This can be achieved by slicing and dicing with a Where clause. An alternative approach involves using criteria with a Filter function. The MDX Where clause is not the same as an SQL one. Hopefully, by the end of the chapter you will be proficient at using it in MDX.

▶ **Key concepts**   Slicing on measures and attributes, filtering on measures and attributes, hiding empty cells, and top and bottom cells

▶ **Keywords**   Where, Except, Filter, Or, And, Is, Not, Non Empty, Topcount, Bottomcount, Toppercent, Bottompercent, Topsum, Bottomsum

Where Clause

We have returned to a "hello world" query. The second query includes an extra Where clause.

Syntax

```
-- hello world again
select
from
[Adventure Works]
-- where slicer, same answer
select
from
[Adventure Works]
where
[Measures].[Reseller Sales Amount]
```

Result

$80,450,596.98

Analysis

Both queries give the same answer. By default, a query uses the default measure to populate the cells with values. The Where clause allows you to slice the cube by a particular measure or dimension attribute or any reasonable combination of measures and/or attributes. It adds extra coordinates to the query—in addition to any coordinates specified as tuples on the Columns and the Rows axes. It works to "narrow down" the results that would otherwise have been returned without it.

Another Measure in a Where Clause

Here are two queries for you to try. The first has a change to the measure in the Where clause. The second projects the measure along the Columns axis.

Syntax

```
-- different answer
select
from
[Adventure Works]
where
[Measures].[Internet Sales Amount]
-- columns rather than where
select
[Measures].[Internet Sales Amount]
on columns
from
[Adventure Works]
```

Result

$29,358,677.22

Internet Sales Amount
$29,358,677.22

Analysis

The cell value from the two queries is the same. However, the second one explicitly lists the measure member on the Columns axis. A Where clause does not project the member onto an axis.

Measure in a Where Clause and on an Axis

But let's try to do both. These two queries are similar, except the second one uses two different measures.

Syntax

```
-- slicer error
select
```

```
[Measures].[Internet Sales Amount]
on columns
from
[Adventure Works]
where
[Measures].[Internet Sales Amount]
-- and again even with different measures
select
[Measures].[Internet Sales Amount]
on columns
from
[Adventure Works]
where
[Measures].[Reseller Sales Amount]
```

Result

```
Executing the query ...
The Measures hierarchy already appears in the Axis0 axis.

Execution complete
```

Analysis

And both produce the same error message. You can't have a member (measure or attribute member) in both the Where clause and on an axis at the same time. Incidentally, Axis0 means the Columns axis.

Default Measure in a Where Clause

Try this query twice. First, run the whole query. Then, highlight everything except the Where clause and run the query again.

Syntax

```
-- default measure as slicer, not needed
select
{[Product].[Product Categories].[Category],[Product].[Product Categories]}
on columns
from
[Adventure Works]
where
[Measures].[Reseller Sales Amount]
```

Result

Accessories	Bikes	Clothing	Components	All Products
$571,297.93	$66,302,381.56	$1,777,840.84	$11,799,076.66	$80,450,596.98

Analysis

It doesn't matter whether or not you include the Where clause when it contains only a default member (measure or attribute). The two queries have identical outcomes. Notice the cell values before you attempt the ensuing query.

A Non-measure Member in the Slicer

Here the slicer has the Canada member of the Customer dimension.

Syntax

```
-- did Canada (customer) have all reseller sales
select
{[Product].[Product Categories].[Category],[Product].
[Product Categories]}
on columns
from
[Adventure Works]
where
[Customer].[Customer Geography].[Country].[Canada]
```

Result

Accessories	Bikes	Clothing	Components	All Products
$571,297.93	$66,302,381.56	$1,777,840.84	$11,799,076.66	$80,450,596.98

Analysis

Identical results to the previous query! But we put Canada into the slicer. Does that mean that all our sales went there? Canadians must be pretty good customers. But not that good—the results are wrong. Customers are not related to Reseller Sales Amount (our default measure here). You will meet this problem if your cube has more than one measure group with differing dimensionalities. We got the wrong dimension with the wrong measure. This is quite important—your reports may show incorrect figures. You need to understand the Dimension Usage tab in your cube designer in BIDS. In the case of Adventure Works, the Sales Territory dimension relates to Reseller Sales

Amount—the Customer dimension relates to Internet Sales Amount. Take a look at the next two queries.

A Non-measure Member in the Slicer (Corrected) 1/2

Still Canada, but the dimension in the slicer is different. It's Sales Territory not Customer.

Syntax

```
-- Canada (sales territory) reseller sales
select
{[Product].[Product Categories].[Category],[Product].
[Product Categories]}
on columns
from
[Adventure Works]
where
[Sales Territory].[Sales Territory].[Country].[Canada]
```

Result

Accessories	Bikes	Clothing	Components	All Products
$118,127.35	$11,636,380.59	$378,947.63	$2,244,470.02	$14,377,925.60

Analysis

Now we have the correct Reseller Sales Amount for Canada.

A Non-measure Member in the Slicer (Corrected) 2/2

Well, the last query worked fine. But what happens if we are interested in Canada as a customer location? The Where clause now includes Canada from the Customer dimension and Internet Sales Amount.

Syntax

```
-- Canada (customer) internet sales
select
{[Product].[Product Categories].[Category],[Product].[Product Categories]}
on columns
```

```
from
[Adventure Works]
where
([Customer].[Customer Geography].[Country].[Canada],
[Measures].[Internet Sales Amount])
```

Result

Accessories	Bikes	Clothing	Components	All Products
$103,377.85	$1,821,302.39	$53,164.62	(null)	$1,977,844.86

Analysis

Once again, we have valid results. There are two members in the slicer. The [Measures].
[Internet Sales Amount] member overrides the default measure of the cube. Notice
the use of a comma and the absence of And. Also, note the parentheses around the two
members. Without the parentheses, there will be a syntax error.

Two Non-measure Members from the Same Dimension Hierarchy

You would like sales to customers in both Canada and Australia, so we add Australia to
the slicer.

Syntax

```
-- Canada/Australia (customer) internet sales
select
{[Product].[Product Categories].[Category],[Product].[Product Categories]}
on columns
from
[Adventure Works]
where
([Customer].[Customer Geography].[Country].[Canada],
[Customer].[Customer Geography].[Country].[Australia],
[Measures].[Internet Sales Amount])
```

Result

```
Executing the query ...
The Customer Geography hierarchy is used more than once in the Crossjoin function.

Execution complete
```

Analysis

What we attempted seemed reasonable. Unfortunately, it doesn't work this way. This error is fixed in the next query.

Two Non-measure Members from the Same Dimension Hierarchy (Fixed)

The only change we make is to delimit the two members from the Customer dimension with braces.

Syntax

```
-- Canada/Australia (customer) internet sales
select
{[Product].[Product Categories].[Category],[Product].[Product Categories]}
on columns
from
[Adventure Works]
where
({[Customer].[Customer Geography].[Country].[Canada],
[Customer].[Customer Geography].[Country].[Australia]},
[Measures].[Internet Sales Amount])
```

Result

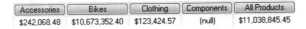

Accessories	Bikes	Clothing	Components	All Products
$242,068.48	$10,673,352.40	$123,424.57	(null)	$11,038,845.45

Analysis

The addition of braces converts Australia and Canada into a set. If you don't do this, SSAS thinks you are asking for a crossjoin. Crossjoins don't work on two members from the same hierarchy.

A Change of Slicer to United Kingdom

Maybe you want to look at reseller sales in the United Kingdom.

Syntax

```
-- UK reseller sales amount
select
```

```
{[Product].[Product Categories].[Category],[Product].[Product Categories]}
on columns
from
[Adventure Works]
where
[Sales Territory].[Sales Territory].[Country].[United Kingdom]
```

Result

Accessories	Bikes	Clothing	Components	All Products
$42,593.03	$3,405,747.21	$118,828.80	$711,839.79	$4,279,008.83

Analysis

There's nothing new here. It's simply a change of the country in the slicer—being careful to use the right dimension with the right measure (the default measure in this case).

Without the United Kingdom

Suppose you now wish to see sales for all countries apart from the United Kingdom. The tedious way is to enumerate every country, without the United Kingdom, in the slicer. These two queries illustrate a very, very convenient alternative.

Syntax

```
-- without the UK
select
{[Product].[Product Categories].[Category],[Product].[Product Categories]}
on columns
from
[Adventure Works]
where
[Sales Territory].[Sales Territory].[Country]
-[Sales Territory].[Sales Territory].[Country].[United Kingdom]
-- or
select
{[Product].[Product Categories].[Category],[Product].[Product Categories]}
on columns
from
[Adventure Works]
where
except([Sales Territory].[Sales Territory].[Country],
[Sales Territory].[Sales Territory].[Country].[United Kingdom])
```

Result

Accessories	Bikes	Clothing	Components	All Products
$528,704.90	$62,896,634.35	$1,659,012.04	$11,087,236.86	$76,171,588.16

Analysis

Our two queries are functionally equivalent and therefore return the same cells. The second query uses the Except set operator whereas the first one uses the minus sign (-), which means Except. Except is covered elsewhere in the book. In effect, it has subtracted the United Kingdom from the list of all the countries in the Sales Territory dimension.

Introducing Filter

The Where clause in MDX bears little resemblance to an SQL Where clause. The nearest you can get to an SQL Where is an MDX Filter function. Before we try it, let's get some dimension attribute members, some measures, and a few cells.

Syntax

```
-- no filter
select
{[Measures].[Internet Sales Amount],[Measures].[Reseller Sales Amount]}
on columns,
[Product].[Product Categories].[Category]
on rows
from
[Adventure Works]
```

Result

	Internet Sales Amount	Reseller Sales Amount
Accessories	$700,759.96	$571,297.93
Bikes	$28,318,144.65	$66,302,381.56
Clothing	$339,772.61	$1,777,840.84
Components	(null)	$11,799,076.66

Analysis

This is going to serve as our starting point for quite a few queries examining the behavior of the Filter function.

A Simple Filter

Let's filter the product categories to hide those with a null (or zero) Internet Sales Amount.

Syntax

```
-- > zero or null
select
{[Measures].[Internet Sales Amount],[Measures].[Reseller Sales Amount]}
on columns,
filter([Product].[Product Categories].[Category],
[Measures].[Internet Sales Amount] > 0)
on rows
from
[Adventure Works]
```

Result

	Internet Sales Amount	Reseller Sales Amount
Accessories	$700,759.96	$571,297.93
Bikes	$28,318,144.65	$66,302,381.56
Clothing	$339,772.61	$1,777,840.84

Analysis

The Components category has been removed from the result set. The first parameter for Filter is the set of members you wish to filter. The second parameter is a Boolean test that returns true or false for each member of the set. Our query stipulates that the Internet Sales Amount must be greater than zero—and Components does not qualify. Nulls in MDX are different from SQL nulls. A null in a numeric cell is also treated as zero. Therefore, the query works even though (if you check back to the last query) the cell for Components contained a null value for Internet sales. This query could also be written with > null rather than > 0 and would give the same result.

As an alternative to the Filter function, you might like to try the Having clause. The Having clause is part of your axis specification and can sometimes simplify the syntax of a query. The syntax of the Having clause looks like this:

```
Select
{[Measures].[Internet Sales Amount],[Measures].[Reseller Sales Amount]}
on columns,
[Product].[Product Categories].[Category]
having [Measures].[Internet Sales Amount] > 0
```

```
on rows
from
[Adventure Works]
```

Another Simple Filter

You might want to see categories that have sales above a certain positive cutoff figure, and not simply those with any sales (which is effectively what the previous query did).

Syntax

```
-- > 500000
select
{[Measures].[Internet Sales Amount],[Measures].[Reseller Sales Amount]}
on columns,
filter([Product].[Product Categories].[Category],
[Measures].[Internet Sales Amount] > 500000)
on rows
from
[Adventure Works]
```

Result

	Internet Sales Amount	Reseller Sales Amount
Accessories	$700,759.96	$571,297.93
Bikes	$28,318,144.65	$66,302,381.56

Analysis

The query asks only for those categories where Internet sales are above $500,000 (or equal to and above if we had used >= instead of >). Not only does it eliminate Components, but also Clothing with Internet sales of $339,772.61 dollars (you can look at the Clothing figure in the result from the last query).

A More Complex Filter with And

Let's make our queries more versatile by having more than one test. Notice the And in the Boolean condition.

Syntax

```
-- using and
select
{[Measures].[Internet Sales Amount],[Measures].[Reseller Sales Amount]}
```

```
on columns,
filter([Product].[Product Categories].[Category],
[Measures].[Internet Sales Amount] > 500000
and [Measures].[Internet Sales Amount] < 750000)
on rows
from
[Adventure Works]
```

Result

	Internet Sales Amount	Reseller Sales Amount
Accessories	$700,759.96	$571,297.93

Analysis

There is only one category (Accessories) where the Internet Sales Amount lies between $500,000 and $750,000. You can make your test condition as complex as you wish, provided you follow the syntax rules.

A More Complex Filter with Or

Sometimes, you may want to exclude a value that lies between other values (note the Or in the test condition).

Syntax

```
-- using or
select
{[Measures].[Internet Sales Amount],[Measures].[Reseller Sales Amount]}
on columns,
filter([Product].[Product Categories].[Category],
[Measures].[Internet Sales Amount] > 750000
 or [Measures].[Internet Sales Amount] < 500000)
on rows
from
[Adventure Works]
```

Result

	Internet Sales Amount	Reseller Sales Amount
Bikes	$28,318,144.65	$66,302,381.56
Clothing	$339,772.61	$1,777,840.84
Components	(null)	$11,799,076.66

Analysis

Our previous query showed only Accessories. This one shows everything but Accessories because its Internet sales at $700,759.96 failed both conditions.

An Even More Complex Filter with And and Or 1/2

You can filter on more than one measure and have both an And and an Or in your test condition. This query may not produce the results you expect!

Syntax

```
-- 2 measures not quite working
select
{[Measures].[Internet Sales Amount],[Measures].[Reseller Sales Amount]}
on columns,
filter([Product].[Product Categories].[Category],
[Measures].[Internet Sales Amount] > 750000
or [Measures].[Internet Sales Amount] < 500000
and [Measures].[Reseller Sales Amount] < 15000000)
on rows
from
[Adventure Works]
```

Result

	Internet Sales Amount	Reseller Sales Amount
Bikes	$28,318,144.65	$66,302,381.56
Clothing	$339,772.61	$1,777,840.84
Components	(null)	$11,799,076.66

Analysis

Look very closely. We have the same result as the previous query. Indeed, the first part of the test condition is identical. The addition tests to see if Reseller Sales Amount is less than $15,000,000. But Bikes is returned, with reseller sales well above that limit. The next query presents a solution.

An Even More Complex Filter with And and Or 2/2

This query is almost identical to the previous one, except it produces a different answer. Note the introduction of parentheses into the test condition.

Syntax

```
-- 2 measures - notice parentheses around the or
select
{[Measures].[Internet Sales Amount],[Measures].[Reseller Sales Amount]}
on columns,
filter([Product].[Product Categories].[Category],
([Measures].[Internet Sales Amount] > 750000
or [Measures].[Internet Sales Amount] < 500000)
and [Measures].[Reseller Sales Amount] < 15000000)
on rows
from
[Adventure Works]
```

Result

	Internet Sales Amount	Reseller Sales Amount
Clothing	$339,772.61	$1,777,840.84
Components	(null)	$11,799,076.66

Analysis

The Bikes category has disappeared. Parentheses help SSAS to understand the order in which to evaluate the result of the test condition. This query is subtly different from the last query in its logic. When you build complex criteria, it's a good idea to add one criterion at a time and double-check the results.

Comparing Two Measures in a Filter

As well as comparing measures against constant values, you can also compare one measure to another measure. This query gives an example.

Syntax

```
-- comparing 2 measures
select
{[Measures].[Internet Sales Amount],[Measures].[Reseller Sales Amount]}
on columns,
filter([Product].[Product Categories].[Category],
[Measures].[Internet Sales Amount]
 > [Measures].[Reseller Sales Amount])
on rows
from
[Adventure Works]
```

Result

	Internet Sales Amount	Reseller Sales Amount
Accessories	$700,759.96	$571,297.93

Analysis

Accessories is the only category where Internet sales surpass reseller sales.

Non-measure Dimension in Filter Test

We are only returning Bikes here. At first sight, the query might appear to be overkill—there are much simpler ways of showing only Bikes. Hopefully, the analysis and the next couple of queries indicate a few possibilities that arise from this approach.

Syntax

```
-- on a non-measure dimension
select
{ [Measures].[Internet Sales Amount],[Measures].[Reseller Sales Amount]}
on columns,
filter([Product].[Product Categories].[Category],
[Product].[Product Categories].currentmember
is [Product].[Product Categories].[Category].[Bikes])
on rows
from
[Adventure Works]
```

Result

	Internet Sales Amount	Reseller Sales Amount
Bikes	$28,318,144.65	$66,302,381.56

Analysis

There are lots of ways of displaying only the Bikes category. The simplest answer is to select only Bikes on the Rows axis. Alternatively, you could include Bikes in a Where slicer. The Filter approach is ultimately much more sophisticated. Unlike Where, Filter surfaces Bikes to appear on an axis. Unlike Where and a simple select, Filter also allows you to use relational operators and establish criteria for measure cutoff points. Note the Is operator and the Currentmember property function.

Two Non-measure Dimensions in Filter Test

Let's continue to build our Filter. Here, we want Bikes and Accessories.

Syntax

```
-- OR operator with a non-measure dimension
select
{[Measures].[Internet Sales Amount],[Measures].[Reseller Sales Amount]}
on columns,
filter([Product].[Product Categories].[Category],
[Product].[Product Categories].currentmember
is [Product].[Product Categories].[Category].[Bikes]
or [Product].[Product Categories].currentmember
is [Product].[Product Categories].[Category].[Accessories])
on rows
from
[Adventure Works]
```

Result

	Internet Sales Amount	Reseller Sales Amount
Accessories	$700,759.96	$571,297.93
Bikes	$28,318,144.65	$66,302,381.56

Analysis

Again, we could have used a simple selection. The power of the Filter lies in its ability to also test for numeric criteria for measures. Hopefully, the next query illustrates why we are persevering with Filter.

Now with Measures Criteria

Suppose we want to see Bikes only if sales are over $1,000,000, and Accessories only if sales are greater than $750,000?

Syntax

```
-- then with a measure condition
select
{[Measures].[Internet Sales Amount],[Measures].[Reseller Sales Amount]}
on columns,
filter([Product].[Product Categories].[Category],
```

```
([Product].[Product Categories].currentmember
is [Product].[Product Categories].[Category].[Bikes]
and [Measures].[Reseller Sales Amount] > 1000000)
or ([Product].[Product Categories].currentmember
is [Product].[Product Categories].[Category].[Accessories])
and [Measures].[Reseller Sales Amount] > 750000)
on rows
from
[Adventure Works]
```

Result

	Internet Sales Amount	Reseller Sales Amount
Bikes	$28,318,144.65	$66,302,381.56

Analysis

Filter test conditions can get quite complex. By breaking the syntax down into parentheses groups, it helps to decipher the syntax. Bikes is shown but Accessories is not. Accessories failed to meet its criterion of $750,000 for reseller sales. This query shows how to use different measure criteria against different dimension members.

Not with Is

How about every category except Clothing? If you recall, you can also do this in a Where clause using the Except function. But here, you can add criteria for your measures as well.

Syntax

```
-- also Not
select
{[Measures].[Internet Sales Amount],[Measures].[Reseller Sales Amount]}
on columns,
filter([Product].[Product Categories].[Category],
not ([Product].[Product Categories].currentmember
is [Product].[Product Categories].[Category].[Clothing]))
on rows
from
[Adventure Works]
```

Result

	Internet Sales Amount	Reseller Sales Amount
Accessories	$700,759.96	$571,297.93
Bikes	$28,318,144.65	$66,302,381.56
Components	(null)	$11,799,076.66

Analysis

You have just seen how to use Not with Is. By combining this with the previous query, you can add very sophisticated filtering to your MDX queries.

Introduction to Non Empty

Rather than use a Filter to weed out zero (null) values, you can try Non Empty. This first query returns all subcategories.

Syntax

```
-- all rows
select
{[Measures].[Internet Sales Amount],[Measures].[Reseller Sales Amount]}
on columns,
[Product].[Product Categories].[Subcategory]
on rows
from
[Adventure Works]
```

Result

	Internet Sales Amount	Reseller Sales Amount
Bike Racks	$39,360.00	$197,736.16
Bike Stands	$39,591.00	(null)
Bottles and Cages	$56,798.19	$7,476.60
Cleaners	$7,218.60	$11,188.37
Fenders	$46,619.58	(null)
Helmets	$225,335.60	$258,712.93
Hydration Packs	$40,307.67	$65,518.75
Lights	(null)	(null)
Locks	(null)	$16,225.22

Analysis

The row for Lights has two zero values in its two cells. SSAS considers a null numeric to be zero (but a value of zero is not considered to be null). You could try a Filter to remove Lights (assuming you do want to hide nulls). Or you might like to experiment with Non Empty (see the next query).

Non Empty

An identical query, almost. All we have done is to introduce Non Empty into the specification for the Rows axis.

Syntax

```
-- Lights disappears
select
{ [Measures].[Internet Sales Amount],[Measures].[Reseller Sales Amount] }
on columns,
non empty [Product].[Product Categories].[Subcategory]
on rows
from
[Adventure Works]
```

Result

	Internet Sales Amount	Reseller Sales Amount
Bike Racks	$39,360.00	$197,736.16
Bike Stands	$39,591.00	(null)
Bottles and Cages	$56,798.19	$7,476.60
Cleaners	$7,218.60	$11,188.37
Fenders	$46,619.58	(null)
Helmets	$225,335.60	$258,712.93
Hydration Packs	$40,307.67	$65,518.75
Locks	(null)	$16,225.22

Analysis

The row for Lights has gone. But, as you can see, Locks survives despite the null entry in the first column. Non Empty works across the whole row. Locks has reseller sales of $16,225.22 and therefore is not empty. If the query had displayed only the Internet Sales Amount column, then Locks would have disappeared, too (you can see this in the next query). Non Empty is covered in more detail elsewhere in the book. But, because it's a kind of filter, it has been included here for completeness.

Tops and Bottoms

Quite often, you will want the best-selling or worst-selling members. Maybe, you would like the top five best-selling subcategories, for instance. This query is a starting point for the next few queries to come.

Syntax

```
-- no tops no bottoms
select
[Measures].[Internet Sales Amount]
on columns,
non empty([Product].[Product Categories].[Subcategory])
on rows
from
[Adventure Works]
```

Result

	Internet Sales Amount
Bike Racks	$39,360.00
Bike Stands	$39,591.00
Bottles and Cages	$56,798.19
Cleaners	$7,218.60
Fenders	$46,619.58
Helmets	$225,335.60
Hydration Packs	$40,307.67
Tires and Tubes	$245,529.32
Mountain Bikes	$9,952,759.56
Road Bikes	$14,520,584.04
Touring Bikes	$3,844,801.05
Caps	$19,688.10
Gloves	$35,020.70
Jerseys	$172,950.68
Shorts	$71,319.81
Socks	$5,106.32
Vests	$35,687.00

Analysis

All records are shown, except those with empty cell values. This is simply a list of all subcategories that have positive Internet sales.

Topcount

First of all, let's just get the top five in the list of subcategories. Here, we take our initial look at the Topcount function.

Syntax

```
-- topcount
select
[Measures].[Internet Sales Amount]
on columns,
non empty(topcount([Product].[Product Categories].[Subcategory],5))
on rows
from
[Adventure Works]
```

Result

	Internet Sales Amount
Bike Racks	$39,360.00
Bike Stands	$39,591.00
Bottles and Cages	$56,798.19
Cleaners	$7,218.60
Fenders	$46,619.58

Analysis

The second parameter is the number 5. All this does is to go and get the first five rows, but it's quite handy when you only want to see a small sample from your set. In this example, the first five rows are those from the top of the previous query result. The order of the rows is not determined by the MDX. Rather, it is determined by the OrderBy property on the Subcategory attribute in BIDS. That property is set to Name, so we have an ascending alphabetical sort.

Topcount with a Measure

Perhaps this is an even more useful query. The measure displayed in the column has been added as a third parameter.

Syntax

```
-- topcount with a measure
select
```

```
[Measures].[Internet Sales Amount]
on columns,
non empty(topcount([Product].[Product Categories].[Subcategory],5,
[Measures].[Internet Sales Amount]))
on rows
from
[Adventure Works]
```

Result

	Internet Sales Amount
Road Bikes	$14,520,584.04
Mountain Bikes	$9,952,759.56
Touring Bikes	$3,844,801.05
Tires and Tubes	$245,529.32
Helmets	$225,335.60

Analysis

When you append the measure as a third parameter to Topcount, it not only gives you five rows, but the contents are for the top five measures in descending sort order. You are looking at the top five best-selling subcategories (in terms of Internet Sales Amount). There is no need to also use the Order function.

Topcount with a Different Measure

The final parameter of Topcount has been replaced with another measure (Reseller Sales Amount), even though we are keeping only Internet Sales Amount on the Columns axis.

Syntax

```
-- with another measure
select
[Measures].[Internet Sales Amount]
on columns,
topcount([Product].[Product Categories].[Subcategory],5,
[Measures].[Reseller Sales Amount])
on rows
from
[Adventure Works]
```

Result

	Internet Sales Amount
Road Bikes	$14,520,584.04
Mountain Bikes	$9,952,759.56
Touring Bikes	$3,844,801.05
Mountain Frames	(null)
Road Frames	(null)

Analysis

This is interesting. Mountain Frames and Road Frames are in our top five, despite zero Internet sales. The criterion for display is, however, reseller sales and not Internet sales.

Topcount with Two Measures

This is the same as the previous query, with the addition of a second measure as a column.

Syntax

```
-- with two measures
select
{[Measures].[Internet Sales Amount],[Measures].[Reseller Sales Amount]}
on columns,
topcount([Product].[Product Categories].[Subcategory],5,
[Measures].[Reseller Sales Amount])
on rows
from
[Adventure Works]
```

Result

	Internet Sales Amount	Reseller Sales Amount
Road Bikes	$14,520,584.04	$29,358,206.96
Mountain Bikes	$9,952,759.56	$26,492,684.38
Touring Bikes	$3,844,801.05	$10,451,490.22
Mountain Frames	(null)	$4,713,672.15
Road Frames	(null)	$3,849,853.34

Analysis

Hopefully, you can now understand why we had Mountain Frames and Road Frames. They are the fourth and fifth best-selling subcategories for reseller sales. Topcount is allowing you to ask to see Internet sales for those subcategories with the best reseller sales.

Bottomcount

How about your worst sellers? This is where Bottomcount comes in useful.

Syntax

```
-- bottomcount
select
[Measures].[Internet Sales Amount]
on columns,
bottomcount([Product].[Product Categories].[Subcategory],30,
[Measures].[Internet Sales Amount])
on rows
from
[Adventure Works]
```

Result

	Internet Sales Amount
Brakes	(null)
Bottom Brackets	(null)
Tights	(null)
Bib-Shorts	(null)
Pumps	(null)
Panniers	(null)
Locks	(null)
Lights	(null)
Socks	$5,106.32
Cleaners	$7,218.60
Caps	$19,688.10
Gloves	$35,020.70
Vests	$35,687.00
Bike Racks	$39,360.00
Bike Stands	$39,591.00
Hydration Packs	$40,307.67
Fenders	$46,619.58
Bottles and Cages	$56,798.19

Analysis

There are lots and lots of nulls at the top. You might have to scroll down through the 30 rows to see the first non-null (Socks).

Bottomcount Hiding the Nulls

Bottomcount returns your worst figures first. Often, this gives lots and lots of nulls—especially if your sales are bad! This query suppresses the nulls.

Syntax

```
-- hiding the nulls, 10 results not 30
select
[Measures].[Internet Sales Amount]
on columns,
non empty bottomcount([Product].[Product Categories].
[Subcategory],30,[Measures].[Internet Sales Amount])
on rows
from
[Adventure Works]
```

Result

	Internet Sales Amount
Socks	$5,106.32
Cleaners	$7,218.60
Caps	$19,688.10
Gloves	$35,020.70
Vests	$35,687.00
Bike Racks	$39,360.00
Bike Stands	$39,591.00
Hydration Packs	$40,307.67
Fenders	$46,619.58
Bottles and Cages	$56,798.19

Analysis

You asked for the bottom 30, but you got only ten. Although this might look a little better, in the real world it might be of vital importance to identify your null (zero) sales and not use Non Empty. The sales are in ascending order. For a descending sort, try an Order function outside the Bottomcount function.

Toppercent

Instead of Topcount or Bottomcount, we are using Toppercent. This is not always an intuitive function to use.

Syntax

```
-- toppercent, 99 returns about half
select
[Measures].[Internet Sales Amount]
on columns,
toppercent([Product].[Product Categories].[Subcategory],99,
[Measures].[Internet Sales Amount])
on rows
from
[Adventure Works]
```

Result

	Internet Sales Amount
Road Bikes	$14,520,584.04
Mountain Bikes	$9,952,759.56
Touring Bikes	$3,844,801.05
Tires and Tubes	$245,529.32
Helmets	$225,335.60
Jerseys	$172,950.68
Shorts	$71,319.81
Bottles and Cages	$56,798.19

Analysis

You are looking at the full cellset. No, it has not returned the top 99 percent of the subcategories. It has resulted in those subcategories whose total Internet sales include 99 percent of the total Internet sales of all the subcategories. It has returned eight subcategories. Shorts is the seventh and Bottles and Cages the eighth. Without Bottles and Cages but with Shorts, the total is less than 99 percent of all sales. Therefore, Bottles and Cages is appended after Shorts, even though we might have over 99 percent of total sales. Toppercent does not add any more rows after the 99 percent is reached or surpassed.

Bottompercent

As you have already guessed, there is also a Bottompercent function.

Syntax

```
-- bottompercent, 1 returns about half
select
[Measures].[Internet Sales Amount]
```

```
on columns,
non empty bottompercent([Product].[Product Categories]
.[Subcategory],1,[Measures].[Internet Sales Amount])
on rows
from
[Adventure Works]
```

Result

	Internet Sales Amount
Socks	$5,106.32
Cleaners	$7,218.60
Caps	$19,688.10
Gloves	$35,020.70
Vests	$35,687.00
Bike Racks	$39,360.00
Bike Stands	$39,591.00
Hydration Packs	$40,307.67
Fenders	$46,619.58
Bottles and Cages	$56,798.19

Analysis

The total sales of these subcategories represent just 1 percent (or possibly just over) of the total sales for all subcategories. All the null values have been suppressed.

Topsum

Here's a variation on a powerful theme, Topsum.

Syntax

```
-- topsum all 3 add up to 26000000
select
[Measures].[Internet Sales Amount]
on columns,
topsum([Product].[Product Categories].[Subcategory],25000000,
[Measures].[Internet Sales Amount])
on rows
from
[Adventure Works]
```

Result

	Internet Sales Amount
Road Bikes	$14,520,584.04
Mountain Bikes	$9,952,759.56
Touring Bikes	$3,844,801.05

Analysis

The second parameter is $25,000,000. The sum of Road Bikes and Mountain Bikes is less than that. If you add on Touring Bikes, the sum is more than that. Therefore, we get our three best-selling subcategories for Internet sales, and together they contribute $25,000,000 (or just over) to our total Internet sales for all subcategories.

Bottomsum

This is the very last query in this chapter. "Last but not least," as they say, even if the function name might suggest otherwise. Here's Bottomsum.

Syntax

```
-- bottomsum
select
[Measures].[Internet Sales Amount]
on columns,
non empty bottomsum([Product].[Product Categories]
.[Subcategory],100000,[Measures].[Internet Sales Amount])
on rows
from
[Adventure Works]
```

Result

	Internet Sales Amount
Socks	$5,106.32
Cleaners	$7,218.60
Caps	$19,688.10
Gloves	$35,020.70
Vests	$35,687.00

Analysis

Excluding nulls, these five subcategories are our worst five, with total sales of only $100,000 (or just over).

Chapter 6

Using the Abacus: Introduction to Calculations

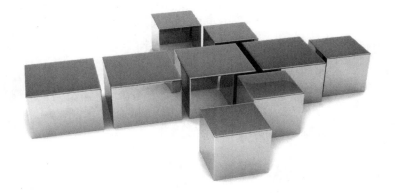

I n general, the measures in your cube are based directly or indirectly on the columns in your fact table in your star schema. However, it's likely your reports will need further metrics. These are often based on the existing measures in some way. One way to devise these new measures is to use MDX query calculations. In this chapter, we explore just how to do this. In addition, we take a look at creating non-measure members and creating our own sets of data.

- ▶ **Key concepts**   Aliases, calculated measures, named sets, formatting, scopes
- ▶ **Keywords**   With Member, format_string, With Set, Create Member, .currentmember, .level, .ordinal

With Clause

So far, to a large extent, we have been using the cube, dimension, hierarchy, and attribute designs that are defined in BIDS. Maybe you design the cubes, or perhaps you inherit and work with cubes designed by others. If you are unable or don't want to alter a design, MDX allows you to extend the cube functionality temporarily by using a With clause before the Select statement. The following few queries give you an introduction to the With clause. A similar clause, Create, will be covered later. The With clause is also useful when you want an ad-hoc, one-off extension to the cube design and it's simply too much to go back and alter the cube in BIDS and then reprocess. Be sure to try this query twice. First, run the whole query including the With clause and the complete Select statement. Then highlight all of the Select statement (and not the With clause) before executing the query again.

Syntax

```
-- hello world calculated member/calculated measure
with member [Measures].[My Measure] as "Hello world"
select
[Measures].[My Measure]
on columns,
[Date].[Calendar].[Calendar Year]
on rows
from
[Adventure Works]
```

Result

	My Measure
CY 2001	Hello world
CY 2002	Hello world
CY 2003	Hello world
CY 2004	Hello world
CY 2006	Hello world

```
Executing the query ...
Query (2, 1) The member '[My Measure]' was not found in the cube when the string, [Measures].[My Measure], was parsed.
Execution complete
```

Analysis

The first run gives you a "Hello world" result. The second attempt produces an error, because the With must be present and run at the same time as the Select statement in order to be referenced. The With clause precedes the Select statement. Note the syntax With Member. You are designing (in code) a calculated member. This particular member has been assigned to the measures dimension ([Measures].[My Measure]) and is called My Measure. When you add a calculated member to your measures, it is called a calculated measure (a subset of calculated members). The calculated measure can only be used in the query of which it's a part. Many people refer to this as a "query-scoped calculation." Should you wish to reuse the calculation in subsequent queries (in the same query editor window), you can replace With with Create. This will give you a session-scoped calculation.

Aliases Through With

Our query demonstrates how to alias an existing measure. Internet Sales Amount has been renamed to Customer Sales. Reseller Sales Amount has been renamed to Retailer Sales.

Syntax

```
-- measure alias
with member [Measures].[Customer Sales] as [Measures]
.[Internet Sales Amount]
member [Measures].[Retailer Sales] as [Measures].[Reseller Sales Amount]
select
{[Measures].[Customer Sales],[Measures].[Retailer Sales]}
on columns,
```

```
[Date].[Calendar].[Calendar Year]
on rows
from
[Adventure Works]
```

Result

	Customer Sales	Retailer Sales
CY 2001	$3,266,373.66	$8,065,435.31
CY 2002	$6,530,343.53	$24,144,429.65
CY 2003	$9,791,060.30	$32,202,669.43
CY 2004	$9,770,899.74	$16,038,062.60
CY 2006	(null)	(null)

Analysis

This aliasing is quite handy when you inherit obscure and unfriendly measure names. There are two calculated measures in this query. Notice the With appears only once and the two Member calculations (albeit very simple calculations!) are not separated by a comma.

Useful Calculations Through With

Okay, perhaps an alias isn't really a calculation as such. This time we do meet a proper calculation. The objective is to return total sales (that is, Internet or customer sales and reseller or retailer sales).

Syntax

```
-- measure calculation
with member [Measures].[Customer Sales] as [Measures]
.[Internet Sales Amount]
member [Measures].[Retailer Sales] as [Measures].[Reseller Sales Amount]
member [Measures].[Total Sales] as [Measures]
.[Internet Sales Amount]+[Measures].[Reseller Sales Amount]
select
{[Measures].[Customer Sales],[Measures].[Retailer Sales],
[Measures].[Total Sales]}
on columns,
[Date].[Calendar].[Calendar Year]
on rows
from
[Adventure Works]
```

Result

	Customer Sales	Retailer Sales	Total Sales
CY 2001	$3,266,373.66	$8,065,435.31	$11,331,808.96
CY 2002	$6,530,343.53	$24,144,429.65	$30,674,773.18
CY 2003	$9,791,060.30	$32,202,669.43	$41,993,729.72
CY 2004	$9,770,899.74	$16,038,062.60	$25,808,962.34
CY 2006	(null)	(null)	(null)

Analysis

The calculated measure here is [Measures].[Total Sales]. It is simply the sum of customer and retailer sales. Even though it's a very basic calculation, the outcome might be just what the end user desires.

Formatting Through With

Quite often, measures are not formatted appropriately in the cube design (FormatString property in BIDS). Sometimes measures are not formatted at all. In addition, if you create your own calculated measures in MDX, you will probably want them formatted in some way. The query here shows you an example, with sales designated in euros.

Syntax

```
-- measure format
with member [Measures].[Total Sales] as [Measures]
.[Internet Sales Amount]+[Measures].[Reseller Sales Amount],
format_string="#,###.00€"
member [Measures].[Customer Sales] as [Measures]
.[Internet Sales Amount],format_string="#,###.00€"
member [Measures].[Retailer Sales] as [Measures]
.[Reseller Sales Amount],format_string="#,###.00€"
select
{[Measures].[Customer Sales],[Measures].[Retailer Sales],
[Measures].[Total Sales]}
on columns,
{[Date].[Calendar].[Calendar Year],[Date].[Calendar]}
on rows
from
[Adventure Works]
```

Result

	Customer Sales	Retailer Sales	Total Sales
CY 2001	3,266,373.66€	8,065,435.31€	11,331,808.96€
CY 2002	6,530,343.53€	24,144,429.65€	30,674,773.18€
CY 2003	9,791,060.30€	32,202,669.43€	41,993,729.72€
CY 2004	9,770,899.74€	16,038,062.60€	25,808,962.34€
CY 2006	(null)	(null)	(null)
All Periods	29,358,677.22€	80,450,596.98€	109,809,274.20€

Analysis

The formatting into euros is defined by format_string="#,###.00€". Notice that it's preceded by a comma (,). The format code is similar to those you may have used in Excel or Visual Basic. There are also named format codes, such as format_string="Percent". A very extensive guide to all the possibilities can be found in Books Online (BOL) by looking up format_string.

With Set 1/2

So far in this chapter, you have seen With Member—a calculated member/calculated measure. MDX also supports With Set. This creates a temporary set that can be used on the axes in the ensuing Select. These are not called calculated sets, as you might have expected. They are called named sets. This query demonstrates using a named set.

Syntax

```
-- with set
with set [Not 2006] as [Date].[Calendar].[Calendar Year]
.[CY 2001]:[Date].[Calendar].[Calendar Year].[CY 2004]
member [Measures].[Total Sales] as [Measures]
.[Internet Sales Amount]+[Measures].[Reseller Sales Amount],
format_string="£#,###.00"
member [Measures].[Customer Sales] as [Measures]
.[Internet Sales Amount],format_string="£#,###.00"
member [Measures].[Retailer Sales] as [Measures]
.[Reseller Sales Amount],format_string="£#,###.00"
select
{[Measures].[Customer Sales],[Measures].[Retailer Sales],
[Measures].[Total Sales]}
on columns,
{[Not 2006],[Date].[Calendar]}
on rows
from
[Adventure Works]
```

Result

	Customer Sales	Retailer Sales	Total Sales
CY 2001	£3,266,373.66	£8,065,435.31	£11,331,808.96
CY 2002	£6,530,343.53	£24,144,429.65	£30,674,773.18
CY 2003	£9,791,060.30	£32,202,669.43	£41,993,729.72
CY 2004	£9,770,899.74	£16,038,062.60	£25,808,962.34
All Periods	£29,358,677.22	£80,450,596.98	£109,809,274.20

Analysis

The named set [Not 2006] is specified for the Rows axis. It shows CY 2001 to CY 2004, inclusive. The range that defines the set is in the With clause. You could have included this range in the Rows specification and not bothered with a named set at all. However, named sets have a number of important uses. For example, they simplify the Select statement and make it easier to read and debug the query. You can create exceedingly complex sets by using one named set as the basis of another named set, and so on.

With Set 2/2

To alert you to possible problems with named sets, have a look at this query. It's identical to the previous query—except in the named set, CY 2004 has been altered to CY 2005.

Syntax

```
-- 2005 doesn't exist
with set [Not 2006] as [Date].[Calendar].[Calendar Year]
.[CY 2001]:[Date].[Calendar].[Calendar Year].[CY 2005]
member [Measures].[Total Sales] as [Measures]
.[Internet Sales Amount]+[Measures].[Reseller Sales Amount],
format_string="£#,###.00"
member [Measures].[Customer Sales] as [Measures]
.[Internet Sales Amount],format_string="£#,###.00"
member [Measures].[Retailer Sales] as [Measures]
.[Reseller Sales Amount],format_string="£#,###.00"
select
{[Measures].[Customer Sales],[Measures].[Retailer Sales],
[Measures].[Total Sales]}
on columns,
{[Not 2006],[Date].[Calendar]}
on rows
from
[Adventure Works]
```

Result

	Customer Sales	Retailer Sales	Total Sales
CY 2001	£3,266,373.66	£8,065,435.31	£11,331,808.96
CY 2002	£6,530,343.53	£24,144,429.65	£30,674,773.18
CY 2003	£9,791,060.30	£32,202,669.43	£41,993,729.72
CY 2004	£9,770,899.74	£16,038,062.60	£25,808,962.34
CY 2006	(null)	(null)	(null)
All Periods	£29,358,677.22	£80,450,596.98	£109,809,274.20

Analysis

Does this look like a strange result? We asked for CY 2001 through CY 2005. Yet CY 2006 has crept into the results. CY 2005 does not exist; therefore, the range starts at CY 2001 but does not have a valid end point. In effect, it keeps going until it falls off the cube and will return all calendar years from CY 2001 onward. I suppose the lesson is to make doubly sure that when you construct named sets you include valid members in the set.

The Scope of With

In order to understand the lifetime or scope of the With clause, consider this query. You might like to try this one a few times, in different ways. First, highlight and run the With section. Second, highlight and run the Select section. Finally, highlight and run both the With section and the Select section. And if you have any patience left, try just the Select by itself.

Syntax

```
-- run the with alone
with member [Measures].[Customer Sales] as [Measures]
.[Internet Sales Amount]
member [Measures].[Retailer Sales] as [Measures].[Reseller Sales Amount]
member [Measures].[Total Sales] as [Measures]
.[Internet Sales Amount]+[Measures].[Reseller Sales Amount]
-- run the select alone
select
{[Measures].[Customer Sales],[Measures].[Retailer Sales],
[Measures].[Total Sales]}
on columns,
[Date].[Calendar].[Calendar Year]
on rows
from
```

```
[Adventure Works]
-- run the with and select together
-- run the select alone one more time
```

Result

```
Executing the query ...
Parser: The end of the input was reached.

Execution complete

Executing the query ...
Query (2, 2) The member '[Customer Sales]' was not found in the cube when the string, [Measures].[Customer Sales], was parsed.

Execution complete
```

	Customer Sales	Retailer Sales	Total Sales
CY 2001	$3,266,373.66	$8,065,435.31	$11,331,808.96
CY 2002	$6,530,343.53	$24,144,429.65	$30,674,773.18
CY 2003	$9,791,060.30	$32,202,669.43	$41,993,729.72
CY 2004	$9,770,899.74	$16,038,062.60	$25,808,962.34
CY 2006	(null)	(null)	(null)

Analysis

We can draw a number of conclusions. You can't run a With without a Select. You can't run a Select without the With that contains the calculated measure that the Select references. Running the With and the Select together works. Subsequent runs of just the Select fail. The calculated measure is query-scoped; it does not survive the first run of the Select. The same argument applies to named sets created by With Set.

The Scope of Create

Create Member gives you a session-scoped calculated member/calculated measure. It can then be reused by multiple Select queries in the *same* query editor window. Create Set for a named set operates in a similar manner. Try the Create by itself first. Then try the Select by itself a couple of times. Finally, run the three Drop Member commands one at a time.

Syntax

```
-- run the Create alone
create member [Adventure Works].[Measures].[Customer Sales] as
[Measures].[Internet Sales Amount]
member [Adventure Works].[Measures].[Retailer Sales] as
[Measures].[Reseller Sales Amount]
```

```
member [Adventure Works].[Measures].[Total Sales] as
[Measures].[Internet Sales Amount]+[Measures].[Reseller Sales Amount]
-- run the Select alone, and a second time
select
{ [Measures].[Customer Sales],[Measures].[Retailer Sales],
[Measures].[Total Sales] }
on columns,
[Date].[Calendar].[Calendar Year]
on rows
from
[Adventure Works]
-- 3 drops
drop member [Adventure Works].[Measures].[Customer Sales]
--
drop member [Adventure Works].[Measures].[Retailer Sales]
--
drop member [Adventure Works].[Measures].[Total Sales]
```

Result

```
Executing the query ...
Execution complete
```

	Customer Sales	Retailer Sales	Total Sales
CY 2001	$3,266,373.66	$8,065,435.31	$11,331,808.96
CY 2002	$6,530,343.53	$24,144,429.65	$30,674,773.18
CY 2003	$9,791,060.30	$32,202,669.43	$41,993,729.72
CY 2004	$9,770,899.74	$16,038,062.60	$25,808,962.34
CY 2006	(null)	(null)	(null)

```
Executing the query ...
Execution complete
```

Analysis

Create Member works alone. The Select works alone (after the Create), and you can run it more than once. Note you can't run the Create and the Select at the same time (unless you place a Go statement just before the Select). The Drop Member removes the session-scoped calculated measure. You should run the three Drop Member commands individually. If you try to run all three together, you will receive an error message (unless you place a Go statement before the second and third ones). After you drop the member/measure, the Select will fail. One very important point to make: When you employ Create Member and Drop Member, you must provide the name of the cube ([Adventure Works].[Measures].[Retailer Sales]). Without the cube name first, both Create Member and Drop Member will fail. But, don't use the cube name in the Select because you will get an error. Instead, simply use [Measures].[Retailer Sales].

Some Classic Calculated Measures

Some calculated measures are implemented over and over again in many organizations. I have called these the classic calculated measures, and they include Percentage of Parent and Percentage of All. The query on this page serves as a starting point for investigating a couple of the classics.

Syntax

```
-- starting point for some classic calculated measure
select
[Measures].[Reseller Sales Amount]
on columns,
{[Product].[Product Categories].[Subcategory].[Mountain Bikes],
[Product].[Product Categories].[Category].[Bikes],
[Product].[Product Categories]}
on rows
from
[Adventure Works]
```

Result

	Reseller Sales Amount
Mountain Bikes	$26,492,684.38
Bikes	$66,302,381.56
All Products	$80,450,596.98

Analysis

The result shows members from three levels of the Product Categories user hierarchy. Mountain Bikes is a subcategory. It belongs to the Bikes category, which, in turn, belongs to the All level member (All Products). We have three generations in the result.

Percentage of Parent 1/2

This is a Percentage of Parent query. If you feel inclined to try it out, you will only be partially successful. With the subsequent query, however, you will be completely successful.

Syntax

```
-- percentage of parent
with member [Measures].[% of parent] as
[Measures].[Reseller Sales Amount]/([Product].[Product Categories]
.currentmember.parent,[Measures]
.[Reseller Sales Amount]),format_string="Percent"
select
{[Measures].[Reseller Sales Amount],[Measures].[% of parent]}
on columns,
{[Product].[Product Categories].[Subcategory].[Mountain Bikes],
[Product].[Product Categories].[Category].[Bikes],
[Product].[Product Categories]}
on rows
from
[Adventure Works]
```

Result

	Reseller Sales Amount	% of parent
Mountain Bikes	$26,492,684.38	39.96%
Bikes	$66,302,381.56	82.41%
All Products	$80,450,596.98	1.#INF

Analysis

Mountain Bikes accounts for 39.96% of the total sales for Bikes. Bikes represents 82.41% of the total reseller sales for all products. Unfortunately, the corresponding cell for All Products doesn't look very nice. In fact, the value in the cell represents infinity. The current member is All Products. The parent of that member does not exist. You can't climb any higher than the All level at the top of a hierarchy. So the sales for the nonexisting parent of All Products are null. SSAS converts the null to zero. A division by zero returns infinity. We need to make this look a little better.

Percentage of Parent 2/2

Hopefully, this result is more pleasing. The All Products cell now shows 100%. Note the use of the .level and .ordinal property functions.

Syntax

```
-- percentage of parent without error
with member [Measures].[% of parent] as
```

```
case when
[Product].[Product Categories].currentmember.level.ordinal = 0
then
1
else
[Measures].[Reseller Sales Amount]/([Product].[Product Categories]
.currentmember.parent,[Measures].[Reseller Sales Amount])
end, format_string="Percent"
select
{[Measures].[Reseller Sales Amount],[Measures].[% of parent]}
on columns,
{[Product].[Product Categories].[Subcategory].[Mountain Bikes],
[Product].[Product Categories].[Category].[Bikes],
[Product].[Product Categories]}
on rows
from
[Adventure Works]
```

Result

	Reseller Sales Amount	% of parent
Mountain Bikes	$26,492,684.38	39.96%
Bikes	$66,302,381.56	82.41%
All Products	$80,450,596.98	100.00%

Analysis

Now the answer is more reasonable. The Case construct tests to see if we are at the top of the hierarchy. If so, it returns 1 and the formatting converts this into 100%. The .level function returns the level of a member. The .ordinal function then returns the level as a number. The All level has an ordinal number of 0 (it is a zero-based index). The sales of All Products are 100% of the sales of All Products, which is perfectly sensible.

Percentage of All

Here's a subtle but important difference from the previous two queries. Here you see how to work out the percentage of the All level.

Syntax

```
-- % of all
with member [Measures].[% of All] as
[Measures].[Reseller Sales Amount]/([Product].[Product Categories]
```

```
.[All],[Measures].[Reseller Sales Amount]),
format_string="Percent"
select
{[Measures].[Reseller Sales Amount],[Measures].[% of All]}
on columns,
{[Product].[Product Categories].[Subcategory].[Mountain Bikes],
[Product].[Product Categories].[Category].[Bikes],
[Product].[Product Categories]}
on rows
from
[Adventure Works]
```

Result

	Reseller Sales Amount	% of All
Mountain Bikes	$26,492,684.38	32.93%
Bikes	$66,302,381.56	82.41%
All Products	$80,450,596.98	100.00%

Analysis

The .currentmember.parent of the previous two queries has been replaced with
a hard-coded reference to the All level. Superficially, the results appear similar. But notice
that the percentage for Mountain Bikes has changed. It is now 32.93% (in the last two
queries it was 39.96%). Mountain Bikes is responsible for 32.93% of all reseller sales for
Adventure Works. Mountain Bikes is also responsible for 39.96% of the sales for Bikes.
The other two percentages remain the same at 82.41% and 100.00%.

Chapter 7

Is Time a Dimension? Working with Dates and Times

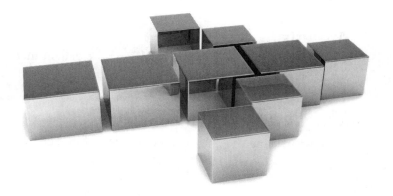

N early every cube in the world has a date or time dimension. MDX provides many rich features that help you to analyze your data across history. In this chapter, you are introduced to lots of functions for manipulating dates and times. These will help you produce brilliant business intelligence reports!

▶ **Key concepts** Date and time manipulation, establishing existing dates, start dates, end dates, and date ranges

▶ **Keywords** .prevmember, .nextmember, ParallelPeriod, ClosingPeriod, OpeningPeriod, null, PeriodsToDate, LastPeriods, YTD, QTD, MTD, WTD

Returning a Specific Fiscal Year

There's really nothing special here. A simple query to get us started on using and navigating time (date) dimensions.

Syntax

```
-- FY 2003 with default measure
select
[Date].[Fiscal].[Fiscal Year].[FY 2003]
on columns
from
[Adventure Works]
```

Result

FY 2003
$27,921,670.52

Analysis

The single cell in the cellset is displaying the default measure (Reseller Sales Amount) for fiscal year (FY) 2003.

The Year Before FY 2003

Here we're using the .prevmember property function.

Syntax

```
-- year before
select
[Date].[Fiscal].[Fiscal Year].[FY 2003].prevmember
on columns
from
[Adventure Works]
```

Result

$16,288,441.77

Analysis

It's an elementary but potentially useful query returning FY 2002.

The Year After

This time it's the .nextmember function.

Syntax

```
-- year after
select
[Date].[Fiscal].[Fiscal Year].[FY 2003].nextmember
on columns
from
[Adventure Works]
```

Result

$36,240,484.70

Analysis

Here we have FY 2004.

A Range of Dates Without a Range Operator

This is a combination of the previous three queries.

Syntax

```
-- previous, FY 2003, and next
select
{[Date].[Fiscal].[Fiscal Year].[FY 2003].prevmember,
[Date].[Fiscal].[Fiscal Year].[FY 2003],
[Date].[Fiscal].[Fiscal Year].[FY 2003].nextmember}
on columns
from
[Adventure Works]
```

Result

FY 2002	FY 2003	FY 2004
$16,288,441.77	$27,921,670.52	$36,240,484.70

Analysis

Here is the Reseller Sales Amount (default measure) for FY 2002, FY 2003, and FY 2004.

Going Back in Time with ParallelPeriod

Here's a query introducing the ParallelPeriod method function.

Syntax

```
-- parallel period previous year
select
parallelperiod([Date].[Fiscal].[Fiscal Year],1,
[Date].[Fiscal].[Fiscal Year].[FY 2003])
on columns
from
[Adventure Works]
```

Result

FY 2002
$16,288,441.77

Analysis

The three parameters are a level, a number, and a member. Go back by the number from the specified member at the specified level. In other words, find the previous year to FY 2003. This is very similar to prevmember and lag, and it has something in common with Cousin. However, ParallelPeriod simplifies your coding when you're creating calculations in queries and in KPIs (more on these, elsewhere in this book) and when you're creating calculations in the cube design in BIDS. The latter are called MDX expressions and are not covered in this book.

Going Forward in Time with ParallelPeriod

The positive number in the last query has been replaced by a negative number.

Syntax

```
-- next year
select
parallelperiod([Date].[Fiscal].[Fiscal Year],-1,
[Date].[Fiscal].[Fiscal Year].[FY 2003])
on columns
from
[Adventure Works]
```

Result

FY 2004
$36,240,484.70

Analysis

Although possibly counterintuitive, a negative number as a parameter to ParallelPeriod takes you forward in time. FY 2004 is returned. You can use ParallelPeriod to help you build ranges.

Too Far into the Future

The numeric parameter this time is −4.

Syntax

```
-- 4 years hence - blank
select
parallelperiod([Date].[Fiscal].[Fiscal Year],-4,
[Date].[Fiscal].[Fiscal Year].[FY 2003])
```

```
on columns
from
[Adventure Works]
```

Result

Analysis
No result at all. Given that the second numeric parameter is −4, you might expect to see FY 2007. Indeed, FY 2007 does exist. The problem is that FY 2006 is missing; therefore, you have to use −3 to see FY 2007. It's vital that your time dimensions contain consecutive and contiguous members (no gaps allowed). Also, a numeric parameter of, say, −25 would take you to years far in the future, which may well exist outside the cube space. You need to be aware of the bounds of your cube space, especially for time dimensions.

How Far into the Future?
Here is the very handy ClosingPeriod method function.

Syntax

```
-- closingperiod
select
closingperiod([Date].[Fiscal].[Fiscal Year])
on columns
from
[Adventure Works]
```

Result

Analysis
FY 2007 is the last fiscal year we have. The (null) in the cell does not indicate that FY 2007 is null or not there. Rather, it shows an empty cell, which means there are no sales for that year, even though the year does exist.

How Far Back?

The opposite of ClosingPeriod is OpeningPeriod.

Syntax

```
-- which is first year
select
openingperiod([Date].[Fiscal].[Fiscal Year])
on columns
from
[Adventure Works]
```

Result

FY 2002
$16,288,441.77

Analysis

FY 2002 is the first fiscal year we have.

Range with OpeningPeriod and Null

Show me the sales for every year up to and including FY 2004.

Syntax

```
-- range with openingperiod
select
openingperiod([Date].[Fiscal].[Fiscal Year]):
[Date].[Fiscal].[Fiscal Year].[FY 2004]
on columns
from
[Adventure Works]
-- range with null
select
null:[Date].[Fiscal].[Fiscal Year].[FY 2004]
on columns
from
[Adventure Works]
```

Result

FY 2002	FY 2003	FY 2004
$16,288,441.77	$27,921,670.52	$36,240,484.70

Analysis

Two queries producing the same cellset. The use of null in the range means "start from just off the edge of the cube space" (just before the first fiscal year, in this case).

Range with ClosingPeriod and Null

Show me the sales for every year after and including FY 2004.

Syntax

```
-- range with closingperiod - from now until end
select
[Date].[Fiscal].[Fiscal Year].[FY 2004]:
closingperiod([Date].[Fiscal].[Fiscal Year])
on columns
from
[Adventure Works]
-- range with null
select
[Date].[Fiscal].[Fiscal Year].[FY 2004]:null
on columns
from
[Adventure Works]
```

Result

FY 2004	FY 2005	FY 2007
$36,240,484.70	(null)	(null)

Analysis

FY 2006 does not exist within the Fiscal Year level.

Range with OpeningPeriod and ClosingPeriod

Now there's no danger of falling off the edge of the cube.

Syntax

```
-- range with openingperiod and closingperiod
select
openingperiod([Date].[Fiscal].[Fiscal Year]):
closingperiod([Date].[Fiscal].[Fiscal Year])
on columns
from
[Adventure Works]
```

Result

FY 2002	FY 2003	FY 2004	FY 2005	FY 2007
$16,288,441.77	$27,921,670.52	$36,240,484.70	(null)	(null)

Analysis

The result shows FY 2002 to FY 2007 (except the missing FY 2006). This is the equivalent of the following:

```
select
[Date].[Fiscal].[Fiscal Year]
on columns
from
[Adventure Works]
```

An Extension to OpeningPeriod

OpeningPeriod is great for returning not only the first member of a level but also the first member within a particular scope. In the two examples that follow, a second member parameter has been added to the OpeningPeriod function.

Syntax

```
-- an extension to openingperiod, calendar
select
openingperiod([Date].[Calendar].[Month],
[Date].[Calendar].[Calendar Year].[CY 2004])
on columns
from
[Adventure Works]
-- an extension to openingperiod, fiscal
select
```

```
openingperiod([Date].[Fiscal].[Month],[Date].[Fiscal].[Fiscal Year]
.[FY 2004])
on columns
from
[Adventure Works]
```

Result

$1,662,547.32

$2,665,650.54

Analysis

The first of the two queries shows the first calendar month in calendar year (CY) 2004. The second query returns the first fiscal month in the fiscal year (FY) 2004. There are, as is usual in MDX, other ways of retrieving the same members. You may find the navigation functions (covered elsewhere in the book) worth investigating.

You must be careful to ensure that the member and level used are from the same hierarchy. The following syntax (which mixes Calendar with Fiscal) will return a date-conversion function error:

```
Select
openingperiod([Date].[Fiscal].[Month],
[Date].[Calendar].[Calendar Year].[CY 2004])
on columns
from
[Adventure Works]
```

Time Gone By

One way to get a range of dates is to use OpeningPeriod with the colon range operator (:). You have just seen an example of this. Perhaps a more convenient and elegant solution involves the PeriodsToDate function.

Syntax

```
-- which years before FY 2004?
select
periodstodate([Date].[Fiscal].[(All)],[Date].[Fiscal].[Fiscal Year]
.[FY 2004])
```

```
on columns
from
[Adventure Works]
-- which months before December 2003 in the same year?
select
periodstodate([Date].[Fiscal].[Fiscal Year],
[Date].[Fiscal].[Month].[December 2003])
on columns
from
[Adventure Works]
```

Result

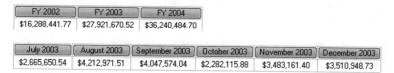

Analysis

Our first result depicts every fiscal year up to and including FY 2004. The second result shows every fiscal month up to and including December 2003 for the fiscal year to which December 2003 belongs. Note that the fiscal year level is the first parameter and December 2003 is the second parameter.

More on Date Ranges with LastPeriods

There is yet another way to establish a date range with the LastPeriods function.

Syntax

```
-- another way, lastperiods, but requires you know 3
select
lastperiods(3,[Date].[Fiscal].[Fiscal Year].[FY 2004])
on columns
from
[Adventure Works]
-- into the future
select
lastperiods(-2,[Date].[Fiscal].[Fiscal Year].[FY 2004])
on columns
from
[Adventure Works]
```

Result

FY 2002	FY 2003	FY 2004
$16,288,441.77	$27,921,670.52	$36,240,484.70

FY 2004	FY 2005
$36,240,484.70	(null)

Analysis

The first parameter for LastPeriods is a numeric value. In the first example, it is 3. This does not mean go back three periods but rather two periods, returning the two periods and the period that is the second parameter, making a total of three. The second example illustrates going forward with a negative number as the first parameter. Thus, it shows FY 2004 and FY 2005.

YTD (Year to Date)

There are even more time functions. This is the YTD (year to date) function.

Syntax

```
-- YTD
select
ytd([Date].[Calendar].[Calendar Quarter].[Q3 CY 2003])
on columns
from
[Adventure Works]
```

Result

Q1 CY 2003	Q2 CY 2003	Q3 CY 2003
$5,266,343.51	$6,733,903.82	$10,926,196.09

Analysis

YTD is simple yet powerful. It accepts only a single parameter, which is optional (it defaults to the current member of the dimension with a Type of Time). Our query shows all the quarters for the current year up to and including the parameter Q3 CY 2003.

YTD Not Working

Sometimes you will encounter errors when working with time functions. This time we fail in order to show you what can go wrong. To help you, a solution is given as well.

Syntax

```
-- YTD broken - use periodstodate
select
ytd([Date].[Fiscal].[Fiscal Quarter].[Q3 FY 2003])
on columns
from
[Adventure Works]
-- workaround
select
periodstodate([Date].[Fiscal].[Fiscal Year],
[Date].[Fiscal].[Fiscal Quarter].[Q3 FY 2003])
on columns
from
[Adventure Works]
```

Result

```
Executing the query ...
Query (2, 1) By default, a year level was expected. No such level was found in the cube.
...
Execution complete
```

Q1 FY 2003	Q2 FY 2003	Q3 FY 2003
$8,880,239.44	$7,041,183.75	$5,266,343.51

Analysis

The last query we tried on YTD worked; it used the Calendar hierarchy in the Date dimension. But it would appear to fail on the Fiscal hierarchy. The Date dimension (or Time dimension, depending on your naming convention) should not be a regular dimension. In the dimension design in BIDS, its Type property must be set to Time. In addition, the attributes of the dimension have a Type property as well. These must be set appropriately for some (but not all) of the time functions to work. For example, YTD requires that the attribute for year has a Type of Years. In the Adventure Works cube, Calendar Year is set to Years and works with YTD. Fiscal Year, on the other hand, is set to FiscalYears and returns an error in this context. BIDS cube and dimension design is beyond the scope of this book, but you may want to consider generating a server time dimension rather than creating your own time dimension in the source star schema. Server time dimensions help to set the Type properties appropriately, both at the dimension and attribute levels. PeriodsToDate is a little more forgiving and returns the results we desire. Be aware that a server time dimension is not always the answer. Server time dimensions have a number of limitations. For example, you can't use the Business Intelligence Wizard in BIDS to add time intelligence to a server time dimension.

QTD (Quarter to Date)

A nice variation on YTD is QTD (quarter to date). This time, two queries are used to show it operating on different levels of the Calendar hierarchy.

Syntax

```
-- QTD for months
select
qtd([Date].[Calendar].[Month].[May 2003])
on columns
from
[Adventure Works]
-- QTD for days
select
[Measures].[Internet Order Count]
on columns,
qtd([Date].[Calendar].[Date].[May 3, 2003])
on rows
from
[Adventure Works]
```

Result

April 2003	May 2003
$1,865,278.43	$2,880,752.68

	Internet Order Count
April 1, 2003	11
April 2, 2003	13
April 3, 2003	5
April 4, 2003	12
April 5, 2003	10
April 6, 2003	5
April 7, 2003	11
April 8, 2003	13
April 9, 2003	10
April 10, 2003	6
April 11, 2003	13

Analysis

So that we don't hit any errors, I have been careful to include the Calendar rather than the Fiscal hierarchy. The two sets of results demonstrate that the xTD functions are sensitive to the level of the member specified as the parameter to the function.

In the second of the two result sets, you may have to scroll down to see the row for May 3, 2003.

MTD (Month to Date)

Another of the xTD functions is MTD (month to date).

Syntax

```
-- MTD
select
mtd([Date].[Calendar].[Date].[July 3, 2003])
on columns
from
[Adventure Works]
```

Result

July 1, 2003	July 2, 2003	July 3, 2003
$2,665,650.54	(null)	(null)

Analysis

After your practice with YTD and QTD, the syntax should be reasonably familiar!

WTD (Week to Date)

Our final time function is WTD (week to date). Unfortunately, the Adventure Works cube does not have an attribute that is a member of the Calendar hierarchy with its Type set to Weeks, so we can expect an error. Apologies for finishing with a failure—however, mistakes often help you learn!

Syntax

```
-- WTD
select
wtd([Date].[Calendar].[Date].[July 3, 2003])
on columns
from
[Adventure Works]
```

Result

```
Executing the query ...
Query (2, 1) By default, a week level was expected. No such level was found in the cube.

Execution complete
```

Analysis

There is an attribute in Adventure Works called Calendar Week with a Type of Weeks, but it is not part of any hierarchy (such as Calendar) that also has the date level. Maybe that's why Books Online (BOL) has examples of YTD, QTD, and MTD, but not WTD. You might want to create your own hierarchy in the Date dimension in BIDS to see this query working.

Chapter 8

Clockwork: Calculations Using Dates and Times

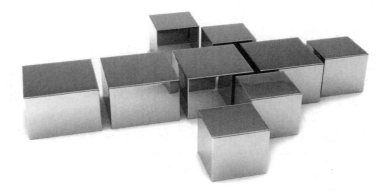

The previous chapter introduced the MDX to extract and manipulate dates. This chapter combines the MDX you learned there with aggregate and other functions. Here you get to use these aggregate and other functions to produce totals, subtotals, and changes across time. This is a big part of business intelligence (BI) reporting.

▶ **Key concepts**   Date and time calculations, increases and decreases, aggregate functions, moving averages, running totals

▶ **Keywords**   ParallelPeriod, IsEmpty, Case, Iif, Sum, Aggregate, Avg, Min, Max, Cousin, .lag, Crossjoin

Calculated Measures with the Time Dimension

Calculated measures are very often used in conjunction with the time dimension of a cube. There are many, many applications. We are going to take a look at a few of the very popular ones. For example, did we have more orders this year than last? This query forms the basis for our examples.

Syntax

```
-- calculated measures with time dimension
select
[Date].[Fiscal].[Fiscal Year]
on columns,
[Measures].[Reseller Order Quantity]
on rows
from
[Adventure Works]
```

Result

	FY 2002	FY 2003	FY 2004	FY 2005	FY 2007
Reseller Order Quantity	21,890	78,959	113,529	(null)	(null)

Analysis

Nothing special here. This is simply to get you started. Subsequent queries build on this one. The result shows Reseller Order Quantity for five fiscal years—FY 2006 does not exist in the cube. FY 2005 and FY 2007 do exist, but no products were sold in either of those two years.

Year-on-Year Growth in Orders

Notice the addition of a new calculated measure on the Rows axis. It shows how order quantities changed from year to year.

Syntax

```
-- increase in orders, year on year
with member [Measures].[Increase] as
([Date].[Fiscal].currentmember,[Measures].[Reseller Order Quantity])
- (ParallelPeriod([Date].[Fiscal].[Fiscal Year],1,[Date].[Fiscal]
.currentmember),[Measures].[Reseller Order Quantity]),format_string="#,#"
select
[Date].[Fiscal].[Fiscal Year]
on columns,
{[Measures].[Reseller Order Quantity],[Measures].[Increase]}
on rows
from
[Adventure Works]
```

Result

	FY 2002	FY 2003	FY 2004	FY 2005	FY 2007
Reseller Order Quantity	21,890	78,959	113,529	(null)	(null)
Increase	21,890	57,069	34,570	-113,529	(null)

Analysis

Our new second row is for a calculated measure called Increase. It compares the order quantity for the current year on the Columns axis with the previous year's order quantity. This is accomplished by using the .currentmember property function and the ParallelPeriod method function. The numeric second parameter for ParallelPeriod is 1. This means "go back one year" (even though it's a positive number, it does not mean "go forward").

Orders Compared to Two Years Ago 1/2

Provided you don't fall off the cube, it's easy to go as far back in time (or forward) as you like to see across-time calculation results. Here we go back two years.

Syntax

```
-- increase from 2 years ago
with member [Measures].[Increase 2 Years] as
([Date].[Fiscal].currentmember,[Measures].[Reseller Order Quantity])
- (ParallelPeriod([Date].[Fiscal].[Fiscal Year],2,[Date].[Fiscal]
.currentmember),[Measures].[Reseller Order Quantity]),format_string="#,#"
select
[Date].[Fiscal].[Fiscal Year]
on columns,
{[Measures].[Reseller Order Quantity],[Measures].[Increase 2 Years]}
on rows
from
[Adventure Works]
```

Result

	FY 2002	FY 2003	FY 2004	FY 2005	FY 2007
Reseller Order Quantity	21,890	78,959	113,529	(null)	(null)
Increase 2 Years	21,890	78,959	91,639	-78,959	-113,529

Analysis

Quite a simple little change—the only difference between this query and the previous one is the numeric second parameter for the ParallelPeriod function. 2 indicates to go back two years and subtract its order quantity from the current year (given by the .currentmember function) to display the increase in orders over a two-year period. Thus, the Increase measure for FY 2004 is 91,639 (113,529 – 21,890). But, maybe, the Increase for FY 2002 and FY 2003 might not be obvious.

Orders Compared to Two Years Ago 2/2

This looks better. The Increase for FY 2002 and FY 2003 now shows NA, rather than a distracting number.

Syntax

```
-- removing first two years
with member [Measures].[Increase 2 Years] as
case
when isempty(ParallelPeriod([Date].[Fiscal].[Fiscal Year],2,[Date]
.[Fiscal].currentmember))
```

```
then "NA"
else
([Date].[Fiscal].currentmember,[Measures].[Reseller Order Quantity]) -
(ParallelPeriod([Date].[Fiscal].[Fiscal Year],2,
[Date].[Fiscal].currentmember),
[Measures].[Reseller Order Quantity])
end,format_string="#,#"
select
[Date].[Fiscal].[Fiscal Year]
on columns,
{[Measures].[Reseller Order Quantity],[Measures].[Increase 2 Years]}
on rows
from
[Adventure Works]
```

Result

	FY 2002	FY 2003	FY 2004	FY 2005	FY 2007
Reseller Order Quantity	21,890	78,959	113,529	(null)	(null)
Increase 2 Years	NA	NA	91,639	-78,959	-113,529

Analysis

The first section of the Case construct tests to see if there is indeed a fiscal year that is two years before the current fiscal year. The IsEmpty function performs the test. If there is no fiscal year two years ago, it returns NA. The output is easier to read and is perhaps what you want. Unless, of course, you are interested in seeing the Increase for FY 2002/FY 2003 since you began trading (both increases are from a null or zero order quantity).

Nulls as Zero 1/2

Some potential improvements can still be made to the last query. A popular tweak is to replace (null) cells with zero. Here you have an attempt to do just that. (Expect this query to fail!)

Syntax

```
-- nulls as zero 1/2
with member [Measures].[Order Quantity] as
iif(isempty([Measures].[Reseller Order Quantity]),0,
[Measures].[Reseller Order Quantity])
member [Measures].[Increase 2 Years] as
case
```

```
when isempty(ParallelPeriod([Date].[Fiscal].[Fiscal Year],2,[Date]
.[Fiscal].currentmember))
then "NA"
else
([Date].[Fiscal].currentmember,[Measures].[Reseller Order Quantity]) -
(ParallelPeriod([Date].[Fiscal].[Fiscal Year],2,
[Date].[Fiscal].currentmember),[Measures].[Reseller Order Quantity])
end,format_string="#,#"
select
[Date].[Fiscal].[Fiscal Year]
on columns,
{[Measures].[Order Quantity],[Measures].[Increase 2 Years]}
on rows
from
[Adventure Works]
```

Result

```
Executing the query ...
The Order Quantity calculated member cannot be created because a member with the same name already exists.

Execution complete
```

Analysis

We have a new calculated measure, Order Quantity. It's designed to convert nulls into zeros. This is attempted by having an Iif test around an IsEmpty one. The new measure replaces the Reseller Order Quantity on the Rows axis. Unfortunately, it generates an error. I suppose I chose a bad name for the measure. If you search the metadata for the Adventure Works cube, you will discover an existing Order Quantity. It is part of the Sales Summary measure group. This is an important point to make—duplicate measure names are not allowed, even if the measures are from different measure groups.

Nulls as Zero 2/2

A simple rename fixes the problem. Our original name (Order Quantity) for the measure is now Quantity Sold. Don't forget to change the entry on the Rows axis as well.

Syntax

```
-- nulls as zero 2/2
with member [Measures].[Quantity Sold] as
iif(isempty([Measures].[Reseller Order Quantity]),0,
[Measures].[Reseller Order Quantity]),format_string="#,#"
```

iPad

On/Off
Sleep/Wak

Silent

Volume
Up/Down

Home

Set up, sync, and charge.

1. Download and install the latest version of iTunes on your Mac or PC from www.itunes.com/download.

2. Connect iPad to your computer using the computer's USB port and the included cable.

3. Follow the onscreen instructions in iTunes to set up iPad and sync your music, movies, TV shows, apps, photos, and more. You can also buy music, movies, and other content from the iTunes Store. Or choose from tens of thousands of apps at the App Store. And if you download the free iBooks app from the App Store, you can buy and read books from the iBookstore.

4. Charge iPad using the included 10W USB Power Adapter.

Learn more.

Find out more about iPad at www.apple.com/ipad.

To view the iPad User Guide on your iPad, tap the bookmark in Safari or go to help.apple.com/ipad.

Visit www.apple.com/support/ipad for technical support. For complete instructions and important safety information, see the iPad User Guide and the Important Product Information Guide at www.apple.com/support/manuals/ipad.

```
member [Measures].[Increase 2 Years] as
case
when isempty(ParallelPeriod([Date].[Fiscal].[Fiscal Year],2,[Date]
.[Fiscal].currentmember))
then "NA"
else
([Date].[Fiscal].currentmember,[Measures].[Reseller Order Quantity]) -
(ParallelPeriod([Date].[Fiscal].[Fiscal Year],2,
[Date].[Fiscal].currentmember),[Measures].[Reseller Order Quantity])
end,format_string="#,#"
select
[Date].[Fiscal].[Fiscal Year]
on columns,
{[Measures].[Quantity Sold],[Measures].[Increase 2 Years]}
on rows
from
[Adventure Works]
```

Result

	FY 2002	FY 2003	FY 2004	FY 2005	FY 2007
Quantity Sold	21,890	78,959	113,529	0	0
Increase 2 Years	NA	NA	91,639	-78,959	-113,529

Analysis

Got there! This is a clear and easily understood result. Over the last few queries, you have learned how to write an MDX query that performs calculations on the time dimension.

Simplifying the Calculation 1/2

There are going to be many occasions when you discover alternative ways of achieving the same result in MDX. This is normally an advantage—you can devise more and more elegant solutions. However, it can create problems, especially when you inherit code written by others. This query and the next one are variations on the last query. The change is subtle and difficult to spot—it's a shorthand that you may find in inherited code.

Syntax

```
-- removing first current member from calculation
with member [Measures].[Quantity Sold] as
iif(isempty([Measures].[Reseller Order Quantity]),0,
```

```
[Measures].[Reseller Order Quantity]),format_string="#,#"
member [Measures].[Increase 2 Years] as
case
when isempty(ParallelPeriod([Date].[Fiscal].[Fiscal Year],2,[Date]
.[Fiscal].currentmember))
then "NA"
else
([Measures].[Reseller Order Quantity]) -
(ParallelPeriod([Date].[Fiscal].[Fiscal Year],2,
[Date].[Fiscal].currentmember),[Measures].[Reseller Order Quantity])
end,format_string="#,#"
select
[Date].[Fiscal].[Fiscal Year]
on columns,
{[Measures].[Quantity Sold],[Measures].[Increase 2 Years]}
on rows
from
[Adventure Works]
```

Result

	FY 2002	FY 2003	FY 2004	FY 2005	FY 2007
Quantity Sold	21,890	78,959	113,529	0	0
Increase 2 Years	NA	NA	91,639	-78,959	-113,529

Analysis

Let's extract a portion of the MDX:

```
([Measures].[Reseller Order Quantity]) -
(ParallelPeriod([Date].[Fiscal].[Fiscal Year],2,
[Date].[Fiscal].currentmember),[Measures].[Reseller Order Quantity])
```

Compare this to our original syntax in the previous query:

```
([Date].[Fiscal].currentmember,[Measures].[Reseller Order Quantity]) -
(ParallelPeriod([Date].[Fiscal].[Fiscal Year],2,
[Date].[Fiscal].currentmember),[Measures].[Reseller Order Quantity]
```

You will notice that the initial reference to [Date].[Fiscal].currentmember has disappeared. If you don't specify the currentmember of the Fiscal hierarchy, it is implicitly assumed.

Simplifying the Calculation 2/2

Here's one more variation on our query. Again, the change is subtle.

Syntax

```
-- removing 2 currentmembers from calculation
with member [Measures].[Quantity Sold] as
iif(isempty([Measures].[Reseller Order Quantity]),0,
[Measures].[Reseller Order Quantity]),format_string="#,#"
member [Measures].[Increase 2 Years] as
case
when isempty(ParallelPeriod([Date].[Fiscal].[Fiscal Year],2,[Date]
.[Fiscal]))
then "NA"
else
([Measures].[Reseller Order Quantity]) -
(ParallelPeriod([Date].[Fiscal].[Fiscal Year],2,
[Date].[Fiscal]),[Measures].[Reseller Order Quantity])
end,format_string="#,#"
select
[Date].[Fiscal].[Fiscal Year]
on columns,
{[Measures].[Quantity Sold],[Measures].[Increase 2 Years]}
on rows
from
[Adventure Works]
```

Result

	FY 2002	FY 2003	FY 2004	FY 2005	FY 2007
Quantity Sold	21,890	78,959	113,529	0	0
Increase 2 Years	NA	NA	91,639	-78,959	-113,529

Analysis

Let's extract a portion of the MDX:

```
([Measures].[Reseller Order Quantity]) -
(ParallelPeriod([Date].[Fiscal].[Fiscal Year],2,
[Date].[Fiscal]),[Measures].[Reseller Order Quantity])
```

Compare this to our original syntax in the previous query:

```
([Date].[Fiscal].currentmember,[Measures].[Reseller Order Quantity]) -
(ParallelPeriod([Date].[Fiscal].[Fiscal Year],2,
[Date].[Fiscal].currentmember),[Measures].[Reseller Order Quantity]
```

You will notice that the second reference to .currentmember has disappeared. If you don't specify the currentmember for a hierarchy, it is implicitly assumed. Indeed, you can even omit the third parameter for ParallelPeriod altogether. In that case, it defaults to the currentmember of the hierarchy of the first parameter. Therefore, the following syntax is also valid:

```
([Date].[Fiscal].currentmember,[Measures].[Reseller Order Quantity]) -
(ParallelPeriod([Date].[Fiscal].[Fiscal Year],2,
[Date].[Fiscal].currentmember),[Measures].[Reseller Order Quantity]
```

Into the Future

How does the quantity sold in a fiscal year differ from that in a subsequent year? This is also a ParallelPeriod query.

Syntax

```
-- into the future
with member [Measures].[Quantity Sold] as
iif(isempty([Measures].[Reseller Order Quantity]),0,
[Measures].[Reseller Order Quantity]),format_string="#,#"
member [Measures].[Change from Next Year] as
([Measures].[Reseller Order Quantity]) - (ParallelPeriod([Date].[Fiscal]
.[Fiscal Year],-1,[Date].[Fiscal]),[Measures].[Reseller Order Quantity]),
format_string="#,#"
select
[Date].[Fiscal].[Fiscal Year]
on columns,
{[Measures].[Quantity Sold],[Measures].[Change from Next Year]}
on rows
from
[Adventure Works]
```

Result

	FY 2002	FY 2003	FY 2004	FY 2005	FY 2007
Quantity Sold	21,890	78,959	113,529	0	0
Change from Next Year	-57,069	-34,570	113,529	(null)	(null)

Analysis

To move into the future, all you have to do is use a negative number (here, it's −1) as the second numeric parameter for the ParallelPeriod function.

A Two-Step Approach

This shows yet another syntactical variation. Here we convert the nulls into zeros again, but this time we adopt a two-step approach.

Syntax

```
-- gets rid of the nulls in cellset
with
member [Measures].[Quantity Sold] as
iif(isempty([Measures].[Reseller Order Quantity]),0,
[Measures].[Reseller Order Quantity]),format_string="#,#"
member [Measures].[Change from Next Year] as
([Measures].[Reseller Order Quantity]) -
(ParallelPeriod([Date].[Fiscal].[Fiscal Year],-1,
[Date].[Fiscal]),[Measures].[Reseller Order Quantity])
member [Measures].[Change] as
iif(isempty([Measures].[Change from Next Year]),0,
[Measures].[Change from Next Year]),format_string="#,#"
select
[Date].[Fiscal].[Fiscal Year]
on columns,
{[Measures].[Quantity Sold],[Measures].[Change]}
on rows
from
[Adventure Works]
```

Result

	FY 2002	FY 2003	FY 2004	FY 2005	FY 2007
Quantity Sold	21,890	78,959	113,529	0	0
Change	-57,069	-34,570	113,529	0	0

Analysis

The second row is the Change measure. This is, of course, a calculated measure. You have already tried a few of these. Only this one is different. The Change measure is based on the Change from Next Year measure. That, in turn, is also a calculated measure. The Change from Next Year is an intermediate measure. You are free to use a calculated measure in another calculated measure. This may simplify the logic and complexity of your code. It's an incremental approach that many MDX people adopt.

Introduction to Sum

So far, we have been examining differences across the time dimension. It's often a requirement to look at totals (for example, a summation) across the time dimension. This query is a starting point for a few examples of what is called aggregation.

Syntax

```
-- SUM
select
{[Date].[Calendar].[Calendar Year].[CY 2001],
[Date].[Calendar].[Calendar Year].[CY 2002]}
 on columns
 from
 [Adventure Works]
 where [Measures].[Internet Order Quantity]
```

Result

CY 2001	CY 2002
1,013	2,677

Analysis

The result is the Internet Order Quantity measure for two calendar years on the Columns axis.

Applying Sum 1/2

This is an interesting query in that, though syntactically valid, the result looks strange—because it is wrong!

Syntax

```
-- incorrect cells
 with member [Date].[Calendar].[Two Years] as
 sum({[Date].[Calendar].[Calendar Year].[CY 2001],
[Date].[Calendar].[Calendar Year].[CY 2002]},
```

```
[Measures].[Internet Order Quantity])
 select
{[Date].[Calendar].[Calendar Year].[CY 2001],
[Date].[Calendar].[Calendar Year].[CY 2002],[Two Years]}
 on columns
 from
 [Adventure Works]
```

Result

CY 2001	CY 2002	Two Years
$8,065,435.31	$24,144,429.65	3,690

Analysis

The Sum function has a set as the first parameter and a measure to aggregate as the second parameter. The Sum function here adds the Internet Order Quantity for CY 2001 and CY 2002. The answer 3,690 is the correct answer. But I forgot to have a Where slicer. CY 2001 and CY 2002 are therefore using the default measure, Reseller Sales Amount. In order to achieve sensible results with aggregation functions such as Sum, it's vital that the query is consistent in its use of measures. Interestingly, the calculated member [Date].[Calendar].[Two Years] has a triple-part name and not a double name, such as [Measures].[Two Years]. It's a calculated member, sure, but not the special case of a calculated measure (more on this in the next query).

Applying Sum 2/2

Hopefully, this is better. Note the inclusion of a Where clause that slices the cube on the Internet Order Quantity measure.

Syntax

```
--where [Measures].[Internet Order Quantity]
 with member [Date].[Calendar].[Two Years] as
 sum({[Date].[Calendar].[Calendar Year].[CY 2001],
[Date].[Calendar].[Calendar Year].[CY 2002]},
[Measures].[Internet Order Quantity])
 select
{[Date].[Calendar].[Calendar Year].[CY 2001],
[Date].[Calendar].[Calendar Year].[CY 2002],[Two Years]}
 on columns
 from
 [Adventure Works]
 where [Measures].[Internet Order Quantity]
```

Result

CY 2001	CY 2002	Two Years
1,013	2,677	3,690

Analysis

This query returns the correct result. It introduces a couple of new concepts. First, it performs an aggregation with the Sum function. Second, it shows the aggregation alongside two members of the Calendar hierarchy on the Columns axis. Members on the same axis have to have the same dimensionality and hierarchality (unless you perform a Crossjoin). The member Two Years is therefore defined as [Date].[Calendar].[Two Years]. Calculated members that are members of the Measures dimension are defined as [Measures].[membername] and are a subset of calculated members, called calculated measures. Calculated members that are not part of the Measures dimension are simply called calculated members and they must be prefaced by both the dimension name and the dimension hierarchy name—here, it's [Date].[Calendar].

Sum Is Not Always Suitable

You have to be careful when using Sum. Sometimes, it can give strange results. The aggregate here is larger than the aggregate in the cube for All Periods.

Syntax

```
-- change to distinct count e.g.
-- [Measures].[Customer Count]
 with member [Date].[Calendar].[Distinct Customers 2003/2004] as
 sum({[Date].[Calendar].[Calendar Year].[CY 2003],
[Date].[Calendar].[Calendar Year].[CY 2004]},[Measures].currentmember)
 select
{[Date].[Calendar].[Calendar Year],[Date].[Calendar],
[Distinct Customers 2003/2004]}
 on columns
 from
 [Adventure Works]
 where [Measures].[Customer Count]
```

Result

CY 2001	CY 2002	CY 2003	CY 2004	CY 2006	All Periods	Distinct Customers 2003/2004
1,013	2,677	9,309	11,377	(null)	18,484	20,686

Analysis

The syntax looks reasonable. It employs the .currentmember property of the Measures dimension in the Sum function, rather than a hard-coded measure name. The property returns the Customer Count measure, which appears in the Where clause. That's a perfectly valid technique. Unfortunately, the calculated member cell is too high at 20,686. It's only for two years, yet the aggregate for all the years (All Periods) is only 18,484. Something is obviously wrong! It's working out the total number of customers for CY 2003 and CY 2004—by adding the two years together. If you have Adventure Works in BIDS and check the Customer Count measure, you will notice that its AggregateFunction property is set to DistinctCount and not to Sum. What we really need is the number of distinct customers in the two years—that's excluding returning customers. The next query shows you how.

In the preceding syntax, [Measures].currentmember is explicitly referenced in the Sum function. You can omit this parameter, if you prefer, because it's implicitly assumed.

Aggregate Function

A small alteration: The Sum function has been replaced with an Aggregate function.

Syntax

```
-- aggregate rather than sum
with member [Date].[Calendar].[Distinct Customers 2003/2004] as
 aggregate({[Date].[Calendar].[Calendar Year].[CY 2003],
[Date].[Calendar].[Calendar Year].[CY 2004]},
[Measures].currentmember)
 select
{[Date].[Calendar].[Calendar Year],[Date].[Calendar],
[Distinct Customers 2003/2004]}
 on columns
 from
[Adventure Works]
 where [Measures].[Customer Count]
```

Result

CY 2001	CY 2002	CY 2003	CY 2004	CY 2006	All Periods	Distinct Customers 2003/2004
1,013	2,677	9,309	11,377	(null)	18,484	18,125

Analysis

The final cell is 18,125. This is the correct answer. The Sum function is a fully additive function. A distinct count is not fully additive—it's not simply a summation. The Aggregate function is safer. It performs the aggregation based on the AggregateFunction setting back in BIDS. If that property is DistinctCount, it will perform a distinct count. If that property is Sum, it will perform a sum. If you don't know the AggregateFunction property setting for a measure, you may want to adopt Aggregate in your MDX.

Sum and Aggregate Together

By combining more than one aggregate function in your MDX syntax, you can arrive at interesting results. This query uses both Sum and Aggregate.

Syntax

```
-- how many customers more than once (repeat customers)
with member [Date].[Calendar].[Repeat Customers 2003/2004] as
 sum({[Date].[Calendar].[Calendar Year].[CY 2003],
[Date].[Calendar].[Calendar Year].[CY 2004]},[Measures].currentmember) -
aggregate({[Date].[Calendar].[Calendar Year].[CY 2003],
[Date].[Calendar].[Calendar Year].[CY 2004]},[Measures].currentmember)
 select
{[Date].[Calendar].[Calendar Year],[Date].[Calendar],
[Repeat Customers 2003/2004]}
 on columns
 from
 [Adventure Works]
 where [Measures].[Customer Count]
```

Result

CY 2001	CY 2002	CY 2003	CY 2004	CY 2006	All Periods	Repeat Customers 2003/2004
1,013	2,677	9,309	11,377	(null)	18,484	2,561

Analysis

The distinct customers for CY 2003 and CY 2004 (Aggregate) are subtracted from the total number of customers (Sum) to give us returning or repeat customers.

More on Sum and Aggregate

We end up with really quite a useful query that has both the Sum and Aggregate functions.

Syntax

```
-- sum and aggregate again
 with member [Date].[Calendar].[Total Customers 2003/2004] as
 sum({[Date].[Calendar].[Calendar Year].[CY 2003],
[Date].[Calendar].[Calendar Year].[CY 2004]},[Measures].currentmember)
 member [Date].[Calendar].[Distinct Customers 2003/2004] as
 aggregate({[Date].[Calendar].[Calendar Year].[CY 2003],
[Date].[Calendar].[Calendar Year].[CY 2004]},[Measures].currentmember)
 member [Date].[Calendar].[Repeat Customers 2003/2004] as
 [Date].[Calendar].[Total Customers 2003/2004]-
[Date].[Calendar].[Distinct Customers 2003/2004]
 select
{[Date].[Calendar].[Calendar Year].[CY 2003],
[Date].[Calendar].[Calendar Year].[CY 2004],[Total Customers 2003/2004],
[Distinct Customers 2003/2004],[Repeat Customers 2003/2004]}
 on columns
 from
 [Adventure Works]
 where [Measures].[Customer Count]
```

Result

CY 2003	CY 2004	Total Customers 2003/2004	Distinct Customers 2003/2004	Repeat Customers 2003/2004
9,309	11,377	20,686	18,125	2,561

Analysis

The repeat customers this time are calculated using two other calculated measures.

Avg Function

Other aggregate functions are available—not just Sum and Aggregate. Here we have the Avg function.

Syntax

```
-- AVG
with member [Date].[Fiscal].[Average] as
avg([Date].[Fiscal].[Fiscal Year],[Measures].[Reseller Sales Amount])
select
non empty { [Date].[Fiscal].[Fiscal Year],[Date].[Fiscal].[Average] }
on columns
from
[Adventure Works]
```

Result

FY 2002	FY 2003	FY 2004	Average
$16,288,441.77	$27,921,670.52	$36,240,484.70	$26,816,865.66

Analysis

The Avg function calculates the average (mean) value. The result shows the average sales across three years. If we had used the Sum function, it would have returned total sales. If we had used the Aggregate function, it would also have given total sales because the AggregateFunction property for Reseller Sales Amount in BIDS is Sum. If you are sure your measure is fully additive, it's normally fine not to use Aggregate. Aggregate will not give you an average if the AggregateFunction is Sum. Instead, Avg will give you an average.

In the example, a measure is used as the second parameter for the Avg function. This can be omitted and Avg will work on the default measure or any measure specified in a Where clause.

Min Function

Which fiscal year (including years with null or zero sales) had the lowest sales? Here we use the Min function.

Syntax

```
-- MIN
with member [Date].[Fiscal].[Minimum] as
min([Date].[Fiscal].[Fiscal Year],[Measures].[Reseller Sales Amount])
select
non empty { [Date].[Fiscal].[Fiscal Year],[Date].[Fiscal].[Minimum] }
on columns
from
[Adventure Works]
```

Result

FY 2002	FY 2003	FY 2004	Minimum
$16,288,441.77	$27,921,670.52	$36,240,484.70	$16,288,441.77

FY 2002	FY 2003	FY 2004	FY 2005	FY 2007	Minimum
$16,288,441.77	$27,921,670.52	$36,240,484.70	(null)	(null)	$16,288,441.77

Analysis

Min returns the minimum value. Try removing Non Empty from the columns specification (which produces the second cellset in the preceding "Result" section). You will then see how Min deals with null values—it does not treat them as zeros as SSAS often does in most other contexts.

Max Function

Max is another aggregate function.

Syntax

```
-- MAX
with member [Date].[Fiscal].[Maximum] as
max([Date].[Fiscal].[Fiscal Year],[Measures].[Reseller Sales Amount])
select
non empty { [Date].[Fiscal].[Fiscal Year],[Date].[Fiscal].[Maximum] }
on columns
from
[Adventure Works]
```

Result

FY 2002	FY 2003	FY 2004	Maximum
$16,288,441.77	$27,921,670.52	$36,240,484.70	$36,240,484.70

Analysis

As you might well expect, Max returns the maximum value.

Moving Average with Avg

The Avg aggregate function (Avg) is frequently employed to generate moving averages.

Syntax

```
-- moving AVG
-- Q4 CY 2006 is not contiguous
with member [Measures].[Moving Average] as
iif(isempty([Date].[Calendar].currentmember.lag(2)),"NA",
avg({[Date].[Calendar].currentmember:[Date].[Calendar].currentmember
.lag(2)},[Measures].[Reseller Order Quantity])),format_string = "#,#"
select
{[Measures].[Reseller Order Quantity],[Measures].[Moving Average]}
on columns,
[Date].[Calendar].[Calendar Quarter]
on rows
from
[Adventure Works]
```

Result

	Reseller Order Quantity	Moving Average
Q3 CY 2001	4,385	NA
Q4 CY 2001	6,450	NA
Q1 CY 2002	4,626	5,154
Q2 CY 2002	6,429	5,835
Q3 CY 2002	27,414	12,823
Q4 CY 2002	19,772	17,872
Q1 CY 2003	12,307	19,831
Q2 CY 2003	19,466	17,182
Q3 CY 2003	39,784	23,852
Q4 CY 2003	28,615	29,288

Analysis

The Lag function and a date range are used in conjunction with Avg to return a moving average across two calendar quarters. The result shown is partial. If you scroll down you will notice Q4 CY 2006. This is not contiguous with the previous quarter and therefore its moving average is arguably incorrect. There are a number of ways of dealing with this. You might employ an IsEmpty test (we did this earlier in this chapter). Or you might want to exclude Q4 CY 2006—you could use the Except operator for this.

The date range has the latest date first—this does not alter the logic in any way. The order of the date range can be reversed without affecting the result. The range would then look like the following (maybe this is easier to read):

```
{[Date].[Calendar].currentmember.lag(2):[Date].[Calendar].currentmember}
```

Sum Giving a Running Total

The aggregate functions can be extended to produce nice results. The previous example showed how to return a moving average. This query demonstrates a running total for sales across calendar years.

Syntax

```
-- running Sum
with member [Measures].[Running Total]
as sum(periodstodate([Date].[Calendar].[(All)],
[Date].[Calendar].currentmember),
[Measures].[Reseller Sales Amount])
select
{[Measures].[Reseller Sales Amount],[Measures].[Running Total]}
on columns,
non empty [Date].[Calendar].[Calendar Year]
on rows
from
[Adventure Works]
```

Result

	Reseller Sales Amount	Running Total
CY 2001	$8,065,435.31	$8,065,435.31
CY 2002	$24,144,429.65	$32,209,864.96
CY 2003	$32,202,669.43	$64,412,534.38
CY 2004	$16,038,062.60	$80,450,596.98
CY 2006	(null)	$80,450,596.98

Analysis

The Sum works across a range of dates returned by the PeriodsToDate function. Notice that Non Empty does not hide CY 2006 because there is a non-null cell entry for the Running Total calculated measure for that year.

Avg Giving a Running Total

This query is very similar to the previous one. Two changes in all. First, we are using Avg rather than Sum. Second, this time YTD is used instead of PeriodsToDate.

Syntax

```
-- avg with ytd
with member [Measures].[Average YTD] as
avg(ytd([Date].[Calendar].currentmember),[Measures]
.[Reseller Sales Amount])
select
descendants([Date].[Calendar].[Calendar Year].[CY 2002],
[Date].[Calendar].[Calendar Quarter])
on columns,
{[Measures].[Reseller Sales Amount],[Measures].[Average YTD]}
on rows
from
[Adventure Works]
```

Result

	Q1 CY 2002	Q2 CY 2002	Q3 CY 2002	Q4 CY 2002
Reseller Sales Amount	$4,069,186.04	$4,153,820.42	$8,880,239.44	$7,041,183.75
Average YTD	$4,069,186.04	$4,111,503.23	$5,701,081.97	$6,036,107.41

Analysis

The result is the average sales for the year up to and including each calendar quarter. This query can be easily adapted to use Sum, Max, or Min.

ParallelPeriod Revisited 1/2

In the last few queries in this chapter, we revisit the ParallelPeriod method function. Sometimes it can give unexpected results. This is certainly something you should be aware of. This query is fine—it uses the Fiscal hierarchy of the Date dimension.

Syntax

```
-- parallelperiod with fiscal
with
member [Measures].[Year Ago] as
case
when isempty(parallelperiod([Date].[Fiscal].[Fiscal Year],1,
[Date].[Fiscal].currentmember)) then "NA"
else
([Measures].[Reseller Sales Amount],
parallelperiod([Date].[Fiscal].[Fiscal Year],1,
```

```
[Date].[Fiscal].currentmember))
end,format_string="Currency"
member [Measures].[Annual Increase] as
iif([Measures].[Year Ago] = "NA","NA",
[Measures].[Reseller Sales Amount] -
[Measures].[Year Ago]),format_string="Currency"
select
{[Measures].[Reseller Sales Amount],
[Measures].[Year Ago],[Measures].[Annual Increase]}
on columns,
nonempty([Date].[Fiscal].[Fiscal Quarter],[Measures]
.[Reseller Sales Amount])
on rows
from
[Adventure Works]
```

Result

	Reseller Sales Amount	Year Ago	Annual Increase
Q1 FY 2002	$3,193,633.97	NA	NA
Q2 FY 2002	$4,871,801.34	NA	NA
Q3 FY 2002	$4,069,186.04	NA	NA
Q4 FY 2002	$4,153,820.42	NA	NA
Q1 FY 2003	$8,880,239.44	$3,193,633.97	$5,686,605.47
Q2 FY 2003	$7,041,183.75	$4,871,801.34	$2,169,382.42
Q3 FY 2003	$5,266,343.51	$4,069,186.04	$1,197,157.47
Q4 FY 2003	$6,733,903.82	$4,153,820.42	$2,580,083.40
Q1 FY 2004	$10,926,196.09	$8,880,239.44	$2,045,956.65
Q2 FY 2004	$9,276,226.01	$7,041,183.75	$2,235,042.26
Q3 FY 2004	$7,102,685.11	$5,266,343.51	$1,836,341.61
Q4 FY 2004	$8,935,377.49	$6,733,903.82	$2,201,473.67

Analysis

This is quite a nice query. The Year Ago calculated measure shows the Reseller Sales Amount for the fiscal quarter one year before the current quarter. The Annual Increase calculated measure then works out the difference. The figures look correct to me. However, they will not always be so—and the next query shows the problem.

ParallelPeriod Revisited 2/2

This is exactly the same query as the last one, except it uses the Calendar hierarchy instead of the Fiscal hierarchy. Indeed, it's only a matter of a simple search and replace—all occurrences of the word *Fiscal* replaced by *Calendar*. The result is wrong!

Syntax

```
-- parallelperiod with calendar
with
member [Measures].[Year Ago] as
case
when isempty(parallelperiod([Date].[Calendar].[Calendar Year],1,
[Date].[Calendar].currentmember)) then "NA"
else
([Measures].[Reseller Sales Amount],
parallelperiod([Date].[Calendar].[Calendar Year],1,[Date].[Calendar]
.currentmember))
end,format_string="Currency"
member [Measures].[Annual Increase] as
iif([Measures].[Year Ago] = "NA","NA",
[Measures].[Reseller Sales Amount] - [Measures].[Year Ago]),
format_string="Currency"
select
{[Measures].[Reseller Sales Amount],[Measures].[Year Ago],
[Measures].[Annual Increase]}
on columns,
nonempty([Date].[Calendar].[Calendar Quarter],
[Measures].[Reseller Sales Amount])
on rows
from
[Adventure Works]
```

Result

	Reseller Sales Amount	Year Ago	Annual Increase
Q3 CY 2001	$3,193,633.97	NA	NA
Q4 CY 2001	$4,871,801.34	NA	NA
Q1 CY 2002	$4,069,186.04	$3,193,633.97	$875,552.07
Q2 CY 2002	$4,153,820.42	$4,871,801.34	($717,980.91)
Q3 CY 2002	$8,880,239.44	NA	NA
Q4 CY 2002	$7,041,183.75	NA	NA
Q1 CY 2003	$5,266,343.51	$4,069,186.04	$1,197,157.47
Q2 CY 2003	$6,733,903.82	$4,153,820.42	$2,580,083.40
Q3 CY 2003	$10,926,196.09	$8,880,239.44	$2,045,956.65
Q4 CY 2003	$9,276,226.01	$7,041,183.75	$2,235,042.26
Q1 CY 2004	$7,102,685.11	$5,266,343.51	$1,836,341.61
Q2 CY 2004	$8,935,377.49	$6,733,903.82	$2,201,473.67

Analysis

Perhaps, instead, I should say that the results are correct given the way ParallelPeriod works. But, to you and me, the Year Ago and Annual Increase calculated measures for all the quarters of CY 2002 appear incorrect. The next few queries will help you understand and arrive at a more satisfactory solution.

Cousin 1/2

Now try this fairly easy MDX using the Cousin function.

Syntax

```
-- cousin 1/2
select
{cousin([Date].[Calendar].[Calendar Quarter].[Q1 CY 2003],
[Date].[Calendar].[Calendar Year].[CY 2002]),
[Date].[Calendar].[Calendar Quarter].[Q1 CY 2003]}
on columns
from
[Adventure Works]
```

Result

Q1 CY 2002	Q1 CY 2003
$4,069,186.04	$5,266,343.51

Analysis

This result is entirely reasonable. We are briefly sidestepping to the Cousin function because it has a similar algorithm to ParallelPeriod but is perhaps easier to decipher. This query is fine; the next one is not.

Cousin 2/2

This is almost the same as the previous query—another look at Cousin. It's worthwhile studying the result, though.

Syntax

```
-- cousin 2/2
select
{cousin([Date].[Calendar].[Calendar Quarter].[Q1 CY 2002],
```

```
[Date].[Calendar].[Calendar Year].[CY 2001]),
[Date].[Calendar].[Calendar Quarter].[Q1 CY 2002]}
on columns
from
[Adventure Works]
```

Result

Q3 CY 2001	Q1 CY 2002
$3,193,633.97	$4,069,186.04

Analysis

Maybe you thought Q1 CY 2001 was a year before Q1 CY 2002, not Q3 CY 2001? Cousin and ParallelPeriod don't quite work that way. They are positional. Q1 CY 2002 is the first quarter in CY 2002. The functions then look for the first quarter in CY 2001. This just happens to be Q3 CY 2001—there is no Q1 CY 2001 (or Q2 CY 2001). The functions are working correctly, but the results are counterintuitive. The problem arises whenever individual members at a parent level have differing numbers of children at a lower level. CY 2002 has four quarters whereas CY 2001 has only two quarters. One solution is to add members Q1 CY 2001 and Q2 CY 2002 with null or zero sales. Other solutions are discussed in the following queries.

Workaround 1/2 Using Lag

Here we've dispensed with ParallelPeriod (and Cousin) and employ the Lag property function instead to go back four quarters (or one year).

Syntax

```
-- workaround 1/2 lag
with
member [Measures].[Year Ago] as
case
when isempty([Date].[Calendar].currentmember.lag(4)) then "NA"
else
([Measures].[Reseller Sales Amount],[Date].[Calendar].currentmember.lag(4))
end,format_string="Currency"
member [Measures].[Annual Increase] as
iif([Measures].[Year Ago] = "NA","NA",
[Measures].[Reseller Sales Amount] -
[Measures].[Year Ago]),format_string="Currency"
select
```

```
{[Measures].[Reseller Sales Amount],
[Measures].[Year Ago],[Measures].[Annual Increase]}
on columns,
nonempty([Date].[Calendar].[Calendar Quarter],
[Measures].[Reseller Sales Amount])
on rows
from
[Adventure Works]
```

Result

	Reseller Sales Amount	Year Ago	Annual Increase
Q3 CY 2001	$3,193,633.97	NA	NA
Q4 CY 2001	$4,871,801.34	NA	NA
Q1 CY 2002	$4,069,186.04	NA	NA
Q2 CY 2002	$4,153,820.42	NA	NA
Q3 CY 2002	$8,880,239.44	$3,193,633.97	$5,686,605.47
Q4 CY 2002	$7,041,183.75	$4,871,801.34	$2,169,382.42
Q1 CY 2003	$5,266,343.51	$4,069,186.04	$1,197,157.47
Q2 CY 2003	$6,733,903.82	$4,153,820.42	$2,580,083.40
Q3 CY 2003	$10,926,196.09	$8,880,239.44	$2,045,956.65
Q4 CY 2003	$9,276,226.01	$7,041,183.75	$2,235,042.26
Q1 CY 2004	$7,102,685.11	$5,266,343.51	$1,836,341.61
Q2 CY 2004	$8,935,377.49	$6,733,903.82	$2,201,473.67

Analysis

Because Lag operates differently from ParallelPeriod (and Cousin), the result is fine. For example, Q1 CY 2002 displays NA in the calculated cells. This is because there is no member that is four back. But even this can break. Take a look at the next query.

Workaround 1/2 Using Lag Breaks

Let's try the previous query again, but this time Non Empty has been removed from the row specification.

Syntax

```
-- workaround 1/2 lag fails for Q4 CY 2006
with
member [Measures].[Year Ago] as
case
when isempty([Date].[Calendar].currentmember.lag(4)) then "NA"
else
```

```
([Measures].[Reseller Sales Amount],[Date].[Calendar].currentmember
.lag(4))
end,format_string="Currency"
member [Measures].[Annual Increase] as
iif([Measures].[Year Ago] = "NA","NA",
[Measures].[Reseller Sales Amount] -
[Measures].[Year Ago]),format_string="Currency"
select
{[Measures].[Reseller Sales Amount],
[Measures].[Year Ago],[Measures].[Annual Increase]}
on columns,
[Date].[Calendar].[Calendar Quarter]
on rows
from
[Adventure Works]
```

Result

	Reseller Sales Amount	Year Ago	Annual Increase
Q3 CY 2001	$3,193,633.97	NA	NA
Q4 CY 2001	$4,871,801.34	NA	NA
Q1 CY 2002	$4,069,186.04	NA	NA
Q2 CY 2002	$4,153,820.42	NA	NA
Q3 CY 2002	$8,880,239.44	$3,193,633.97	$5,686,605.47
Q4 CY 2002	$7,041,183.75	$4,871,801.34	$2,169,382.42
Q1 CY 2003	$5,266,343.51	$4,069,186.04	$1,197,157.47
Q2 CY 2003	$6,733,903.82	$4,153,820.42	$2,580,083.40
Q3 CY 2003	$10,926,196.09	$8,880,239.44	$2,045,956.65
Q4 CY 2003	$9,276,226.01	$7,041,183.75	$2,235,042.26
Q1 CY 2004	$7,102,685.11	$5,266,343.51	$1,836,341.61
Q2 CY 2004	$8,935,377.49	$6,733,903.82	$2,201,473.67
Q3 CY 2004	(null)	$10,926,196.09	($10,926,196.09)
Q4 CY 2006	(null)	$9,276,226.01	($9,276,226.01)

Analysis

Lag works for all the rows except the last one. The two calculated cells for Q4 CY 2006 are incorrect. In the last query, Non Empty suppressed Q4 CY 2006. This time, however, it's displayed. Four back from Q4 CY 2006 is actually Q4 CY 2003 and not Q4 CY 2005. Hopefully, you've learned some very important lessons, especially for working with time dimensions. One, members of each level should have an equal number of children at the next level down. Two, members should be contiguous—no gaps. A server time dimension can help avoid some of these problems. If (as it is in the real world) your data is not perfect, attempt the next query.

Workaround 2/2 Using Crossjoin

If your data is not contiguous, you might want to combine a Crossjoin with the ParallelPeriod function.

Syntax

```
-- workaround 2/2 crossjoin
with member [Measures].[Year Ago] as
([Measures].[Reseller Sales Amount],
Parallelperiod([Date].[Calendar].[Calendar Year],1,
[Date].[Calendar].currentmember)),format_string = "Currency"
select
{[Measures].[Reseller Sales Amount],[Measures].[Year Ago]} on columns,
crossjoin([Date].[Calendar Year].[Calendar Year],
[Date].[Calendar Quarter of Year].[Calendar Quarter of Year])
on rows
from
[Adventure Works]
```

Result

		Reseller Sales Amount	Year Ago
CY 2001	CY Q3	$3,193,633.97	(null)
CY 2001	CY Q4	$4,871,801.34	(null)
CY 2002	CY Q1	$4,069,186.04	(null)
CY 2002	CY Q2	$4,153,820.42	(null)
CY 2002	CY Q3	$8,880,239.44	$3,193,633.97
CY 2002	CY Q4	$7,041,183.75	$4,871,801.34
CY 2003	CY Q1	$5,266,343.51	$4,069,186.04
CY 2003	CY Q2	$6,733,903.82	$4,153,820.42
CY 2003	CY Q3	$10,926,196.09	$8,880,239.44
CY 2003	CY Q4	$9,276,226.01	$7,041,183.75
CY 2004	CY Q1	$7,102,685.11	$5,266,343.51
CY 2004	CY Q2	$8,935,377.49	$6,733,903.82
CY 2004	CY Q3	(null)	$10,926,196.09
CY 2006	CY Q4	(null)	(null)

Analysis

This should always give you the desired results. The Crossjoin forces ParallelPeriod to behave as you might expect it.

Chapter 9

Venn Diagrams: Visualizing and Manipulating Sets

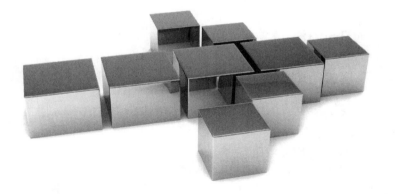

T his is a wide-ranging chapter on working with sets and members of sets. By the end of the chapter, you'll be able to create, visualize, and manipulate sets.

▶ **Key concepts** Named sets, joining sets, set operations, extracting members, missing members, member properties, visual totals

▶ **Keywords** Distinct, .item, Generate, Rank, Union, Intersect, Except, With Set, Head, Subset, Tail, VisualTotals, Create Set, Extract, Exists, Count, .count

Distinct

When you have duplicate members returned by a query, you can suppress the duplicates with Distinct. Here are two queries for you to try.

Syntax

```
-- distinct 1/2
select { [Geography].[Country].[Australia],[Geography].[Country]
.[Australia]}
on columns
from
[Adventure Works]
-- distinct 2/2
select distinct { [Geography].[Country].[Australia],
[Geography].[Country].[Australia]}
on columns
from
[Adventure Works]
```

Result

Analysis

Not terribly useful as it stands—you are unlikely to ask for Australia twice. However, this chapter includes many advanced set operations, and the members returned are not always explicitly defined. In those cases, Distinct is very handy for removing duplication in the result.

Item on a Set

The Item property member performed against a set returns a tuple within the set. What is the third calendar year in our Date dimension?

Syntax

```
-- item on a set returns a tuple
select
[Date].[Calendar].[Calendar Year].item(2)
on columns
from
[Adventure Works]
-- alternative (2)Syntax
select
[Date].[Calendar].[Calendar Year].members(2)
on columns
from
[Adventure Works]
```

Result

CY 2003
$32,202,669.43

Analysis

Both queries give the same result. Here we are returning the third calendar year. Item is zero based.

Item on a Tuple

Sometimes you may want to select a particular item (based on position) within a tuple.

Syntax

```
-- item on a tuple returns a member
select
([Date].[Calendar].defaultmember,
[Product].[Product Categories].defaultmember).item(1)
on columns
from
[Adventure Works]
```

Result

Analysis

The tuple has two members. Item is zero based and .item(1) returns the second member, which is All Products.

Generate

If you want to perform the same operation against two or more sets, Generate may be of help.

Syntax

```
-- generate
with set [Bikes and Clothing] as
{[Product].[Product Categories].[Category].[Bikes],
[Product].[Product Categories].[Category].[Clothing]}
set [Two Families] as
generate({[Bikes and Clothing]},
[Product].[Product Categories].currentmember.children)
select
[Two Families]
on columns
from
[Adventure Works]
```

Result

Mountain Bikes	Road Bikes	Touring Bikes	Bib-Shorts	Caps	Gloves	Jerseys	Shorts	Socks	Tights	Vests
$26,492,684.38	$29,358,206.96	$10,451,490.22	$166,739.71	$31,541.35	$207,775.17	$579,308.71	$342,202.72	$24,638.81	$201,833.01	$223,801.37

Analysis

Generate is not the easiest of the MDX syntax. Here, Generate creates a set called Two Families, which is projected along the Columns axis. Generate operates on a set called Bikes and Clothing and returns the children of that set. This is quite useful because .children normally only works directly on an individual member, not a set. By using Generate, we are able to have .children apply against the members in the Bikes and Clothing set one at a time. The result is all the children of both Bikes and Clothing.

Rank

Where do we sell the most, and what position is each city in the rankings?

Syntax

```
-- rank
with set [Countries and Cities] as
{crossjoin([Customer].[Country].[Country],filter([Customer].[City].[City],
[Measures].[Internet Sales Amount] > 0))}
member [Measures].[Ranking] as
rank([Customer].[City].currentmember,
[Customer].[City].currentmember.siblings,[Measures]
.[Internet Sales Amount])
select
{[Measures].[Internet Sales Amount],[Measures].[Ranking]}
on columns,
order([Countries and Cities],[Measures].[Internet Sales Amount],bdesc)
on rows
from
[Adventure Works]
```

Result

		Internet Sales Amount	Ranking
United Kingdom	London	$802,810.30	1
France	Paris	$539,725.80	2
Australia	Wollongong	$338,913.47	3
Australia	Warrnambool	$327,036.37	4
Australia	Bendigo	$314,568.72	5
Australia	Goulburn	$310,875.90	6
United States	Bellflower	$302,278.81	7
Australia	Brisbane	$295,353.58	8

Analysis

An Order function is used to sort the rows with the highest sales at the top. The result of the Rank function is shown in the second column. Rank compares a city against all its siblings. For example, Bendigo in Australia comes in at number 5. If the third parameter for Rank is omitted, the ranking is based on the position of the first parameter in the second set parameter; in this case, Bendigo comes in at number 31.

Union, Intersect, Except Base Query 1/2

Some of the fundamental set operators are Union, Intersect, and Except. To investigate their use, we need two base queries. This is the first of the two.

Syntax

```
-- best cities in 2003
with set [Best Cities in CY 2003] as
order(topcount([Customer].[Customer Geography].[City],10,
([Measures].[Internet Sales Amount],
[Date].[Calendar].[Calendar Year].[CY 2003])),
[Measures].[Internet Sales Amount],bdesc)
select
[Measures].[Internet Sales Amount]
on columns,
[Best Cities in CY 2003]
on rows
from
[Adventure Works]
where [Date].[Calendar].[Calendar Year].[CY 2003]
```

Result

	Internet Sales Amount
London	$336,223.71
Paris	$233,163.14
Wollongong	$123,579.77
Bendigo	$116,121.34
Warrnambool	$112,847.99
Hobart	$106,911.35
Melton	$103,427.66
Goulburn	$98,667.35
Townsville	$95,656.38
Melbourne	$95,591.56

Analysis

The result shows the ten best cities, in terms of Internet sales, for CY 2003. In this and the next few queries, the Order function is redundant. By default, Topcount will sort in descending order and break any hierarchies. Conversely, Bottomcount will sort in ascending order. You might want to use Order to force an ascending sort on Topcount (or a descending sort on Bottomcount).

Union, Intersect, Except Base Query 2/2

This is the second of our two base queries.

Syntax

```
-- best cities in 2004
with set [Best Cities in CY 2004] as
order(topcount([Customer].[Customer Geography].[City],10,
([Measures].[Internet Sales Amount],
[Date].[Calendar].[Calendar Year].[CY 2004])),
[Measures].[Internet Sales Amount],bdesc)
select
[Measures].[Internet Sales Amount]
on columns,
[Best Cities in CY 2004]
on rows
from
[Adventure Works]
where [Date].[Calendar].[Calendar Year].[CY 2004]
```

Result

	Internet Sales Amount
London	$286,474.92
Paris	$175,338.19
Bellflower	$116,752.62
Wollongong	$99,650.02
Brisbane	$95,118.98
Berkeley	$92,682.88
Sydney	$90,781.20
Burlingame	$89,550.19
Bendigo	$88,268.71
Townsville	$87,999.40

Analysis

The result shows our ten best cities for CY 2004. Note the list of top cities for CY 2004 is slightly different from the list for CY 2003 (shown in the previous query).

Union

Maybe you want the two lists of cities in one result—the best cities for CY 2003 and CY 2004. The query has the Union set operator.

Syntax

```
-- two years together
with set [Best Cities in CY 2003/2004] as
union(order(topcount([Customer].[Customer Geography].[City],10,
([Measures].[Internet Sales Amount],
[Date].[Calendar].[Calendar Year].[CY 2003])),
[Measures].[Internet Sales Amount],bdesc),
order(topcount([Customer].[Customer Geography].[City],10,
([Measures].[Internet Sales Amount],
[Date].[Calendar].[Calendar Year].[CY 2004])),
[Measures].[Internet Sales Amount],bdesc))
select
[Measures].[Internet Sales Amount]
on columns,
[Best Cities in CY 2003/2004]
on rows
from
[Adventure Works]
where {[Date].[Calendar].[Calendar Year].[CY 2003]
,[Date].[Calendar].[Calendar Year].[CY 2004]}
```

Result

	Internet Sales Amount
London	$622,698.63
Paris	$408,501.33
Wollongong	$223,229.79
Bendigo	$204,390.05
Warrnambool	$200,055.66
Townsville	$183,655.78
Goulburn	$181,467.83
Hobart	$160,153.91
Melton	$158,670.16
Melbourne	$153,198.24
Bellflower	$186,720.94
Sydney	$185,763.40
Brisbane	$179,821.51
Berkeley	$168,084.73
Burlingame	$150,504.95

Analysis

We started with two lists of ten cities each for the two years. Union has put them together, but there are not 20 cities in the result—there are only 15. If a city appears in both of the lists, it appears only once after the Union (there is an optional ALL third parameter to Union that retains duplicates). For example, London was our best city in both CY 2003 and CY 2004, yet the union only shows it once. The sales figure is the total for the two years.

Intersect

Which cities were in our top ten in both years? Here, the set operator is Intersect.

Syntax

```
-- intersect, cities in both years
with set [Best Cities in CY 2003/2004] as
intersect(order(topcount([Customer].[Customer Geography].[City],10,
([Measures].[Internet Sales Amount],
[Date].[Calendar].[Calendar Year].[CY 2003])),
[Measures].[Internet Sales Amount],bdesc),
order(topcount([Customer].[Customer Geography].[City],10,
([Measures].[Internet Sales Amount],
[Date].[Calendar].[Calendar Year].[CY 2004])),
[Measures].[Internet Sales Amount],bdesc))
select
[Measures].[Internet Sales Amount]
on columns,
[Best Cities in CY 2003/2004]
on rows
from
[Adventure Works]
where {[Date].[Calendar].[Calendar Year].[CY 2003],
[Date].[Calendar].[Calendar Year].[CY 2004]}
```

Result

	Internet Sales Amount
London	$622,698.63
Paris	$408,501.33
Wollongong	$223,229.79
Bendigo	$204,390.05
Townsville	$183,655.78

Analysis

Five cities (including London) were in our top ten for both years.

Except 1/2

Which cities dropped out of the top ten from one year to the next? Here we have the Except operator.

Syntax

```
-- except these dropped out
with set [Best Cities in CY 2003/2004] as
except(order(topcount([Customer].[Customer Geography].[City],10,
([Measures].[Internet Sales Amount],
[Date].[Calendar].[Calendar Year].[CY 2003])),
[Measures].[Internet Sales Amount],bdesc),
order(topcount([Customer].[Customer Geography].[City],10,
([Measures].[Internet Sales Amount],
[Date].[Calendar].[Calendar Year].[CY 2004])),
[Measures].[Internet Sales Amount],bdesc))
select
[Measures].[Internet Sales Amount]
on columns,
[Best Cities in CY 2003/2004]
on rows
from
[Adventure Works]
where {[Date].[Calendar].[Calendar Year].[CY 2003]}
```

Result

	Internet Sales Amount
Warrnambool	$112,847.99
Hobart	$106,911.35
Melton	$103,427.66
Goulburn	$98,667.35
Melbourne	$95,591.56

Analysis

A couple of important points are worth making. CY 2003 appears in the Where slicer. CY 2003 precedes CY 2004 within the Except. These are the CY 2003 cities that did not make it as CY 2004 cities.

Except 2/2

This, in a way, is the reverse of the previous query. Which cities were in our top ten in CY 2004 that had not been in our top ten in CY 2003?

Syntax

```
-- except these entered in 2004
with set [Best Cities in CY 2003/2004] as
except(order(topcount([Customer].[Customer Geography].[City],10,
([Measures].[Internet Sales Amount],
[Date].[Calendar].[Calendar Year].[CY 2004])),
[Measures].[Internet Sales Amount],bdesc),
order(topcount([Customer].[Customer Geography].[City],10,
([Measures].[Internet Sales Amount],
[Date].[Calendar].[Calendar Year].[CY 2003])),
[Measures].[Internet Sales Amount],bdesc)
)
select
[Measures].[Internet Sales Amount]
on columns,
[Best Cities in CY 2003/2004]
on rows
from
[Adventure Works]
where {[Date].[Calendar].[Calendar Year].[CY 2004]}
```

Result

	Internet Sales Amount
Bellflower	$116,752.62
Brisbane	$95,118.98
Berkeley	$92,682.88
Sydney	$90,781.20
Burlingame	$89,550.19

Analysis

This time we have CY 2004 in the Where clause and CY 2004 precedes CY 2003 within the Except. It's probably a good idea to spend some time comparing this query with the previous one.

Head

Here are two queries and two cellsets demonstrating the use of the Head function.

Syntax

```
-- head first one
select
head([Date].[Fiscal].[Fiscal Quarter],1)
on columns
from
[Adventure Works]
-- head first two
select
head([Date].[Fiscal].[Fiscal Quarter],2)
on columns
from
[Adventure Works]
```

Result

Q1 FY 2002
$3,193,633.97

Q1 FY 2002	Q2 FY 2002
$3,193,633.97	$4,871,801.34

Analysis

Head with a parameter of 1 is the same as .Item(0). (Technically, there is a difference in that Head returns a set of one item and .Item simply returns an item.) .Item is zero based and returns one tuple/member from a set. Head is one based and can return multiple members. The second result shows the first two quarters in the Fiscal Quarter hierarchy.

Subset

Show me the second fiscal quarter followed by the next two quarters. This query introduces Subset.

Syntax

```
-- second quarter then the next two
select
subset([Date].[Fiscal].[Fiscal Quarter],1,3)
on columns
from
[Adventure Works]
```

Result

Q2 FY 2002	Q3 FY 2002	Q4 FY 2002
$4,871,801.34	$4,069,186.04	$4,153,820.42

Analysis

Subset takes two numeric parameters. The first parameter is the start position of a member. The second parameter is the number of members to return. The parameters are not intuitive. Subset (like .Item and unlike Head) starts at zero. Thus, our query starts at the second fiscal quarter. The second parameter is how many members to return, including the first member.

Tail

You wish to display the last two fiscal quarters. This is the Tail function.

Syntax

```
-- tail
select
tail([Date].[Fiscal].[Fiscal Quarter],2)
on columns
from
[Adventure Works]
```

Result

Q1 FY 2005	Q2 FY 2007
(null)	(null)

Analysis

If you omit the second numeric parameter for Tail, it defaults to 1. The same applies to Head.

Subset with Count

Count gives you the number of members in a set. Here it's combined with Subset.

Syntax

```
-- fifth last then two more
select
subset([Date].[Fiscal].[Fiscal Quarter],
[Date].[Fiscal].[Fiscal Quarter].count-5,3)
on columns
from
[Adventure Works]
```

Result

Q2 FY 2004	Q3 FY 2004	Q4 FY 2004
$9,276,226.01	$7,102,685.11	$8,935,377.49

Analysis

Count-5 returns the fifth last member. Then we show a total of three members including that one.

Nonvisual Totals

A normal MDX Select shows any totals as nonvisual totals. This query has the total for All Periods and the values that help make up that total for three individual calendar years.

Syntax

```
-- non visual totals
select
{[Date].[Calendar],[Date].[Calendar].[Calendar Year].[CY 2002]:
[Date].[Calendar].[Calendar Year].[CY 2004]}
on columns
from
[Adventure Works]
```

Result

All Periods	CY 2002	CY 2003	CY 2004
$80,450,596.98	$24,144,429.65	$32,202,669.43	$16,038,062.60

Analysis

The query deliberately omitted two calendar years. However, if you add the values for the three years shown and subtract that from the All Periods total, you can work out the combined value for the two missing years.

Visual Totals

This may be the preferable behavior. The figure for All Periods is different from the last query. In SSAS and MDX, this is known as a visual total.

Syntax

```
-- visual totals
select
visualtotals({[Date].[Calendar],[Date].[Calendar].[Calendar Year]
.[CY 2002]:[Date].[Calendar].[Calendar Year].[CY 2004]})
on columns
from
[Adventure Works]
```

Result

All Periods	CY 2002	CY 2003	CY 2004
$72,385,161.68	$24,144,429.65	$32,202,669.43	$16,038,062.60

Analysis

Notice the all-important change to the value for All Periods. This is achieved by the VisualTotals function. Now it's impossible to figure out the combined sales for the two missing calendar years. If this is the behavior you want, you must specify it. Subselects and subcubes (introduced in the next chapter) are exactly the opposite. By default, subselects and subcubes use visual totals. Should you want nonvisual totals in subselects and subcubes, you have to explicitly ask for them.

Note that the reference to All Periods must come first. The following query does not produce the same result:

```
Select
visualtotals({[Date].[Calendar].[Calendar Year].[CY 2002]:
[Date].[Calendar].[Calendar Year].[CY 2004],[Date].[Calendar]})
on columns
from
[Adventure Works]
```

Named Sets 1/2

Named sets simplify your columns or rows specification in the Select part of the query. Here the named set is Europe.

Syntax

```
-- with set - gives a named set
with set [Europe] as
{[Customer].[Customer Geography].[Country].[France],
[Customer].[Customer Geography].[Country].[Germany],
[Customer].[Customer Geography].[Country].[United Kingdom]}
select
[Europe]
on columns
from
[Adventure Works]
where [Measures].[Internet Sales Amount]
```

Result

France	Germany	United Kingdom
$2,644,017.71	$2,894,312.34	$3,391,712.21

Analysis

With Set is query scoped. You can't reuse [Europe] in another query, unless you repeat the With Set.

Named Sets 2/2

Here are three queries for you to try. Be sure to run them separately. The result shown is for the Select query only.

Syntax

```
-- create set - gives a set
create set [Adventure Works].[Europe] as
{[Customer].[Customer Geography].[Country].[France],
[Customer].[Customer Geography].[Country].[Germany],
[Customer].[Customer Geography].[Country].[United Kingdom]}
-- select from named set
select
[Europe]
on columns
from
[Adventure Works]
where [Measures].[Internet Sales Amount]
-- drop set
drop set [Adventure Works].[Europe]
```

Result

France	Germany	United Kingdom
$2,644,017.71	$2,894,312.34	$3,391,712.21

Analysis

If you wanted, before you dropped the named set, you could run the Select again or write another Select query (in the same query editor window) that specified [Europe] on its columns or rows. Create Set is session scoped.

MeasureGroupMeasures

You can create a set of measures members by listing each measure individually. However, if all the measures belong to the same measure group, the following is a convenient shorthand.

Syntax

```
-- all measures in a measure group as a set
select MeasureGroupMeasures("Internet Sales") on columns
from
[Adventure Works]
```

Result

Internet Sales Amount	Internet Order Quantity	Internet Extended Amount	Internet Tax Amount	Internet Freight Cost	Internet Total Product Cost	Internet Standard Product Cost
$29,358,677.22	60,398	$29,358,677.22	$2,348,694.23	$733,969.61	$17,277,793.58	$17,277,793.58

Analysis

Notice that this function requires the name of a measure group and not that of a measure. In addition, the measure group name has to be in quotes—both single and double quotes work. Measure groups are part of your cube design back in BIDS. A measure group usually (but not necessarily always) corresponds to a fact table in the source relational star schema database. Both star schema and cube design are beyond the scope of an MDX query book.

Extract 1/2

If you have a series of complex set operations that returns a crossjoin, you may be interested in removing just one hierarchy from that crossjoin. This is where Extract might be useful. The following is a base query for the Extract shown in the next query.

Syntax

```
-- extract reversing a crossjoin 1/2
select
crossjoin([Reseller].[Reseller Type].[Business Type],
{[Product].[Product Categories].[Bikes],
[Product].[Product Categories].[Clothing]})
on columns
from
[Adventure Works]
```

Result

Specialty Bike Shop	Specialty Bike Shop	Value Added Reseller	Value Added Reseller	Warehouse	Warehouse
Bikes	Clothing	Bikes	Clothing	Bikes	Clothing
$6,080,117.73	$252,933.91	$30,892,354.33	$592,385.71	$29,329,909.50	$932,521.23

Analysis

Hopefully you are beginning to feel comfortable with crossjoins.

Extract 2/2

Note that the Extract appears outside the Crossjoin function.

Syntax

```
-- extract reversing a crossjoin 2/2
select
extract(crossjoin([Reseller].[Reseller Type].[Business Type],
{[Product].[Product Categories].[Category].[Bikes],
[Product].[Product Categories].[Category].[Clothing]}),
[Product].[Product Categories])
on columns
from
[Adventure Works]
```

Result

Bikes	Clothing
$66,302,381.56	$1,777,840.84

Analysis

The Extract function has returned the members of the Product Categories hierarchy from the Crossjoin function.

Sorting Non-measure Dimensions 1/4

Elsewhere in the book, you saw how to sort cells using the Order function. We sorted them on the values of measures (for example, sorting by decreasing sales). This and the next few queries introduce you to a different kind of sorting—sorting sets of members alphabetically.

Syntax

```
-- alphabetical sort on product subcategory breaking
-- hierarchy
select
[Measures].[Reseller Sales Amount]
on columns,
order([Product].[Product Categories].[Subcategory],
[Product].[Product Categories].currentmember.member_name,bdesc)
on rows
from
[Adventure Works]
```

Result

	Reseller Sales Amount
Wheels	$679,070.07
Vests	$223,801.37
Touring Frames	$1,642,327.69
Touring Bikes	$10,451,490.22
Tires and Tubes	$925.21
Tights	$201,833.01
Socks	$24,638.81
Shorts	$342,202.72
Saddles	$55,829.39
Road Frames	$3,849,853.34
Road Bikes	$29,358,206.96
Pumps	$13,514.69
Pedals	$147,483.91
Panniers	(null)
Mountain Frames	$4,713,672.15
Mountain Bikes	$26,492,684.38

Analysis

The subcategories are sorted alphabetically in descending order (using .currentmember .member_name). Also, the sort ignores the hierarchy—the category to which a subcategory belongs is ignored (Bdesc).

Sorting Non-measure Dimensions 2/4

This example has no explicit Order function. Yet, there does appear to be some ordering—at least some of the rows.

Syntax

```
-- ordering within hierarchies 1/2
select
[Measures].[Reseller Sales Amount]
on columns,
{ [Product].[Product Categories].[Category],
[Product].[Product Categories].[Subcategory]}
on rows
from
[Adventure Works]
```

Result

	Reseller Sales Amount
Accessories	$571,297.93
Bikes	$66,302,381.56
Clothing	$1,777,840.84
Components	$11,799,076.66
Bike Racks	$197,736.16
Bike Stands	(null)
Bottles and Cages	$7,476.60
Cleaners	$11,188.37
Fenders	(null)
Helmets	$258,712.93
Hydration Packs	$65,518.75
Lights	(null)
Locks	$16,225.22
Panniers	(null)
Pumps	$13,514.69
Tires and Tubes	$925.21
Mountain Bikes	$26,492,684.38

Analysis

Here we asked for categories first—Accessories, Bikes, Clothing, and Components. These are arranged alphabetically, without an explicit Order function that is controlled by the OrderBy property in BIDS. Here it happens to be set to Name. Then we requested subcategories. These are sorted alphabetically up to a point. Notice the two rows for Tires and Tubes and Mountain Bikes cause the sort to stop working. The sort on subcategories does not break the hierarchy. Tires and Tubes is part of Accessories, and Mountain Bikes is part of Bikes. Within the hierarchy, the sort is dictated by the OrderBy property in BIDS—again it's Name. The next query demonstrates a different approach.

Sorting Non-measure Dimensions 3/4

Possibly, this looks better. Accessories is no longer followed by Bikes, another category. Rather, Accessories is followed by the subcategories in Accessories—before Bikes and its own subcategories begin. The categories appear in alphabetical order, as do the subcategories within their own categories.

Syntax

```
-- ordering within hierarchies 2/2
select
[Measures].[Reseller Sales Amount]
on columns,
```

```
order({[Product].[Product Categories].[Category],
[Product].[Product Categories].[Subcategory]},
[Product].[Product Categories].currentmember.member_name)
on rows
from
[Adventure Works]
```

Result

	Reseller Sales Amount
Accessories	$571,297.93
Bike Racks	$197,736.16
Bike Stands	(null)
Bottles and Cages	$7,476.60
Cleaners	$11,188.37
Fenders	(null)
Helmets	$258,712.93
Hydration Packs	$65,518.75
Lights	(null)
Locks	$16,225.22
Panniers	(null)
Pumps	$13,514.69
Tires and Tubes	$925.21
Bikes	$66,302,381.56
Mountain Bikes	$26,492,684.38

Analysis

The Order function here operates not on one level but on two levels, Category and Subcategory. This is achieved by converting Category and Subcategory members into a single set by using braces. The sort is alphabetic using .currentmember.member_name.

Sorting Non-measure Dimensions 4/4

This is a nice variation on the previous query. We are still sorting within hierarchies but in combination with a traditional Order on a measure.

Syntax

```
-- ordering within hierarchies and by measure
select
[Measures].[Reseller Sales Amount]
on columns,
order({[Product].[Product Categories].[Category],
[Product].[Product Categories].[Subcategory]},
```

```
[Measures].[Reseller Sales Amount],desc)
on rows
from
[Adventure Works]
```

Result

	Reseller Sales Amount
Bikes	$66,302,381.56
Road Bikes	$29,358,206.96
Mountain Bikes	$26,492,684.38
Touring Bikes	$10,451,490.22
Components	$11,799,076.66
Mountain Frames	$4,713,672.15
Road Frames	$3,849,853.34
Touring Frames	$1,642,327.69
Wheels	$679,070.07
Cranksets	$203,942.62

Analysis

Here we have sorted by category and by subcategory within each category on the Reseller Sales Amount. For example, Road Bikes and Mountain Bikes are no longer in alphabetical sequence. Also note that Accessories is no longer the first category—you will have to scroll down to see it.

Dimension Properties

For once, we don't have measures in our first column. An occupation such as Clerical is not a measure—it's a dimension attribute member. The Occupation attribute is related to the Customer attribute hierarchy—it is not part of the same hierarchy. When attributes are related this way, they are called member properties. Because they also live in the same dimension, they are also referred to as dimension properties.

Syntax

```
-- dimension properties
with member [Measures].[Occupation] as
[Customer].[Customer].currentmember.properties("occupation")
select
{[Measures].[Occupation],[Measures].[Internet Order Count]}
on columns,
[Customer].[Customer].[Customer]
on rows
```

```
from
[Adventure Works]
where
[Customer].[Customer Geography].[State-Province].[South Australia]
```

Result

	Occupation	Internet Order Count
Adrienne Gutierrez	Skilled Manual	2
Adrienne Ruiz	Manual	2
Alan Lu	Clerical	1
Albert R. Alvarez	Professional	2
Alfredo Ruiz	Professional	1
Alicia L. Beck	Professional	2
Alicia Yuan	Professional	2
Alisha Chander	Manual	2
Alisha E. Beck	Management	3
Alison Chander	Management	2
Alvin Jai	Skilled Manual	2

Analysis

We have an interesting result that is ideal for BI reports. Note the syntax
.currentmember.properties("occupation"). Member properties are set up in BIDS when
you create an attribute relationship between two attributes and those two attributes do
not participate in a user hierarchy. Attribute relationship design is beyond the scope
of this book, but you don't need BIDS to see them. They are visible in your MDX
query editor in SSMS. You might want to try this: In the Metadata pane, expand the
Customer dimension, then the Customer attribute hierarchy, then the Customer level
in that hierarchy, and finally the Member Properties folder in that level. You should see
Occupation in the list of member properties. The following query produces the same
result (in certain circumstances, it may even perform better):

```
with member [Measures].[Occupation] as
[Customer].[Occupation].currentmember.name
select
{[Measures].[Occupation],[Measures].[Internet Order Count]}
on columns,
[Customer].[Customer].[Customer]
on rows
from
[Adventure Works]
where
[Customer].[Customer Geography].[State-Province].[South Australia]
```

Sorting by Dimension Properties

Maybe you want to sort your customers by occupation. Yes, it is possible to order on a member property.

Syntax

```
-- ordering by dimension property
with member [Measures].[Occupation] as
[Customer].[Customer].currentmember.properties("occupation")
select
{[Measures].[Occupation],[Measures].[Internet Order Count]}
on columns,
order([Customer].[Customer].[Customer],[Measures].[Occupation],asc)
on rows
from
[Adventure Works]
where
[Customer].[Customer Geography].[State-Province].[South Australia]
```

Result

	Occupation	Internet Order Count
Neil Jimenez	Clerical	1
Phillip Suri	Clerical	2
Raquel W. Hernandez	Clerical	2
Robyn O. Ramos	Clerical	2
Roger F. Lu	Clerical	2
Shawn Shen	Clerical	2
Tammy L. Arthur	Clerical	1
Tanya Moreno	Clerical	2
Alisha E. Beck	Management	3
Alison Chander	Management	2
Andre H. Garcia	Management	3

Analysis

This is quite a useful technique. First, the member property is converted to a measure, [Measures].[Occupation]. Second, the Order function uses that measure as the basis for the sort.

Missing Member Caused by a Typo

Sometimes your sets may include missing members. These may be caused either by typos or by not understanding a member's position in a hierarchy. Both are easily done, so it's good to be aware of the problem and how to stop it happening. The next few queries investigate further.

Syntax

```
-- missing member due to a typo
select
{[Customer].[Customer Geography].[Country].[United Kingdom],
[Customer].[Customer Geography].[Country].[UK]}
on columns
from
[Adventure Works]
where [Measures].[Internet Sales Amount]
```

Result

United Kingdom
$3,391,712.21

Analysis

Oops, a typo. There is a country called United Kingdom in the country level, but not one called UK. You can spot this by observing that UK simply doesn't show.

Missing Member Caused by a Non-Typo 1/2

The problem here is harder to identify. Is it a typo I made or a logic error of some kind? If you expand the Metadata pane, you can see that Quebec is a valid member of the State-Province level.

Syntax

```
-- missing member due to a non-typo on one axis
select
crossjoin({[Customer].[Customer Geography].[Country].[United Kingdom]},
{[Customer].[State-Province].[Quebec],
[Customer].[State-Province].[England]})
on columns
```

```
from
[Adventure Works]
where [Measures].[Internet Sales Amount]
```

Result

Analysis

Quebec has disappeared. This is not a typo. I simply wasn't aware that Quebec is maybe not in the United Kingdom! Let's try it on two axes rather than one.

Missing Member Caused by a Non-Typo 2/2

Instead of a crossjoin on one axis, let's see what happens to Quebec when we use two axes. So, there is no crossjoin this time.

Syntax

```
-- missing member due to a non-typo on two axes
select
{[Customer].[Customer Geography].[Country].[United Kingdom]}
on columns,
{[Customer].[State-Province].[Quebec],[Customer].[State-Province]
.[England]}
on rows
from
[Adventure Works]
where [Measures].[Internet Sales Amount]
```

Result

Analysis

Quebec is back. This result is quite strange—it would seem to show that Quebec is in the United Kingdom, only sales were not very good there. Not sure what's happening here. To those of you who like looking at maps, after I wrote this query I discovered a tiny village called Quebec in the United Kingdom! By Quebec, I mean the Quebec that is a province of Canada and is at the State-Province level.

Hiding Non-Typo Missing Members 1/2

This is a preferable result. Note the inclusion of the Exists function.

Syntax

```
-- missing member suppressed by exists
select
{[Customer].[Customer Geography].[Country].[United Kingdom]}
on columns,
exists({[Customer].[State-Province].[Quebec],
[Customer].[State-Province].[England]},
{[Customer].[Customer Geography].[Country].[United Kingdom]}
)
on rows
from
[Adventure Works]
where [Measures].[Internet Sales Amount]
```

Result

Analysis

The Exists function is checking to see if Quebec and England are children of the United Kingdom. It only returns the ones (in this case, only England) that evaluate to true. If we had had Scotland in the dimension, that would have appeared even if it had null sales.

Hiding Non-Typo Missing Members 2/2

An alternative approach is simply to have a Where clause in the MDX.

Syntax

```
-- missing member suppressed by where clause
select
```

```
{ [Customer].[State-Province].[Quebec],[Customer].[State-Province]
.[England] }
on columns
from
[Adventure Works]
where (([Measures].[Internet Sales Amount],
[Customer].[Customer Geography].[Country].[United Kingdom])
```

Result

England
$3,391,712.21

Analysis

This works fine, too. Perhaps the Exists version is a little more elegant, and it allows us to see United Kingdom in the grid.

More on Exists 1/3

This is a really careless query—easily done when you don't know the data well. Because cubes can contain millions of members, it's not difficult to build meaningless sets as is done here.

Syntax

```
-- Mountain-100 Black, 44 is not in Components
select   [Product].[Category].[Components] on columns,
{ [Product].[Product].[Product].[ML Fork],
[Product].[Product].[Product].[Chain],
[Product].[Product].[Mountain-100 Black, 44] }
on rows
from
[Adventure Works]
```

Result

	Components
ML Fork	(null)
Chain	$9,377.71
Mountain-100 Black, 44	(null)

Analysis

Chain is in Components. ML Fork is in Components with null sales. Mountain-100 Black, 44 is in Bikes not Components. Our results are wrong!

More on Exists 2/3

Let's try and get rid of Mountain-100 Black, 44 with a clever Non Empty.

Syntax

```
-- but ML Fork is!
select  [Product].[Category].[Components] on columns,
non empty {[Product].[Product].[Product].[ML Fork],
[Product].[Product].[Product].[Chain],
[Product].[Product].[Mountain-100 Black, 44]}
on rows
from
[Adventure Works]
```

Result

Analysis

That's cool—Mountain-100 Black, 44 has gone. Chain is indeed a child of Components, but it's still not right. ML Fork, which is in Components, has gone, too. The next query fixes this.

More on Exists 3/3

Here's one final attempt at solving the riddle of missing members. Non Empty has been replaced by the Exists function.

Syntax

```
-- ML Fork
select  [Product].[Category].[Components] on columns,
exists({[Product].[Product].[Product].[ML Fork],
[Product].[Product].[Product].[Chain],
```

```
[Product].[Product].[Mountain-100 Black, 44]},
[Product].[Category].[Components])
on rows
from
[Adventure Works]
```

Result

	Components
ML Fork	(null)
Chain	$9,377.71

Analysis

We got there at last. ML Fork is a child of Components (even if sales were pretty bad). The purpose of this query (using Exists) and the previous query (using Non Empty) is to illustrate the subtle but vital difference between Non Empty and Exists. When you suspect missing members are not caused by typos, then Exists is a safe bet.

Counting Members in a Set

Here's quite a common request: How many customers do we have? We need to establish the number of members in a set. There are two ways of counting. Two queries to run separately.

Syntax

```
-- how many customers? 1/2
with member [Measures].[Customers] as
count([Customer].[Customer].[Customer])
select
[Measures].[Customers]
on columns
from
[Adventure Works]
-- how many customers? 2/2
with member [Measures].[Customers] as
[Customer].[Customer].[Customer].count
select
[Measures].[Customers]
on columns
from
[Adventure Works]
```

Result

Analysis

Same result from both queries: There are 18,484 customers. First, we used the Count method function. Second, we used the .count property function.

Chapter 10

Views on Cubes:
Working with Subcubes

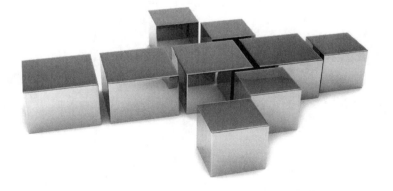

I f you are familiar with SQL, you may use views. One use of a view on a relational table is to present only a part of the table. Often, you will want to work on only a part of a cube. The SSAS versions of SQL views are called perspectives, subselects, and subcubes. In this chapter we get to exploit those perspectives, subselects, and subcubes.

► **Key concepts**   Views on cubes, visual totals

► **Keywords**   Select, Non Visual, .defaultmember, Create Subcube

Select from a Perspective

These two queries are only relevant if you have the Enterprise edition of SSAS (you may want to move on to the next query if you don't have the Enterprise edition). The Enterprise edition supports an aspect of cube design called a perspective. The Standard edition does not include support for perspectives. A perspective reveals only a portion of the cube to your MDX queries. Perspectives are created at design time back in BIDS and their design is beyond the scope of this book. If you do have perspectives, they can be seen in the Perspectives tab of your cube design. A perspective is analogous to a single-table view on a relational database. Perspectives are related to the virtual cubes feature of Analysis Services 2000. They differ from subselects and subcubes. Subselects and subcubes (discussed in the next few queries) are created in your MDX; perspectives are predefined.

Syntax

```
-- select from a perspective
select
[Measures].[Internet Sales Amount]
on columns
from
[Direct Sales]
select
[Measures].[Reseller Sales Amount]
on columns
from
[Direct Sales]
```

Result

Internet Sales Amount
$29,358,677.22

Analysis

If you attempted both the queries, you will see that the preceding result only occurs with the first query. The second query returns absolutely nothing. The reason is that Internet Sales Amount is a measure included in the perspective (Direct Sales), whereas Reseller Sales Amount is not, even though the latter is part of the larger Adventure Works cube. Notice we are not using the cube name in the From clause.

Base Query for Subselects

A subselect is a Select within a Select. Subselects are analogous to subqueries in SQL. Before we embark on a short tour of subselects, here's a base query.

Syntax

```
-- base query for subselect
select
[Sales Reason].[Sales Reasons].[Reason Type]
on columns
from
[Adventure Works]
where [Measures].[Internet Sales Amount]
```

Result

Marketing	Other	Promotion
$27,475.82	$18,678,948.02	$6,361,828.95

Analysis

Nothing complicated. But note the value ($18,678,948.02) in the cell for sale reason Other.

Subselect 1/2

A subselect requires that you replace the cube name in the From clause with another complete and self-contained Select. The inner Select must be self-standing—that is, it will function as a query if run by itself.

Syntax

```
-- subselect 1/2
select
```

```
[Sales Reason].[Sales Reasons].[Reason Type]
on columns
from
(select
[Sales Reason].[Sales Reasons].[Reason Type].[Other]
on columns
from
[Adventure Works]
)
where [Measures].[Internet Sales Amount]
```

Result

Other
$18,678,948.02

Analysis

The subselect restricts the outer query to only seeing the sales reason type Other. The other reason types are not available to the outer query. Note that the Where clause is outside the subselect and slices on Internet Sales Amount.

Subselect 2/2

This version of the previous subselect is subtly different. It's going to return an invalid result—the Sales Reason dimension is not related to the Reseller Sales measure group in the cube design. If you are familiar with BIDS, take a look at the IgnoreUnrelatedDimensions property for measure groups—you can use that to suppress the cell value.

Syntax

```
-- subselect 2/2
select
[Sales Reason].[Sales Reasons].[Reason Type]
on columns
from
(select
[Sales Reason].[Sales Reasons].[Reason Type].[Other]
on columns
from
[Adventure Works]
where [Measures].[Internet Sales Amount])
```

Result

Analysis

The single cell displays the Reseller Sales Amount and not the Internet Sales Amount. In this version, the Where slicer is inside the subselect and not part of the outer query (contrast this with the last query). The outer query does not specify any measure, so the default measure (Reseller Sales Amount) is applied. This may be counterintuitive, but it's how subselects work and it's worth knowing.

Visual Totals

Subselects, by default, use an SSAS feature called visual totals. If you are an SSAS administrator and get involved in cube and dimension security, you might have already met visual totals. It really is a clever concept.

Syntax

```
-- visual totals
select
{[Date].[Calendar],[Date].[Calendar].[Calendar Year].members}
on columns
from
(select [Date].[Calendar].[Calendar Year].[CY 2002]:
[Date].[Calendar].[Calendar Year].[CY 2004] on columns
from [Adventure Works])
```

Result

All Periods	CY 2002	CY 2003	CY 2004
$72,385,161.68	$24,144,429.65	$32,202,669.43	$16,038,062.60

Analysis

The subselect suppresses two years (CY 2001 and CY 2006). The All Periods total is the total for only those years allowed in the subselect. There is no way of deducing the possible sales for the two missing years.

Nonvisual Totals

Note the use of Non Visual between the From and the subselect.

Syntax

```
-- non-visual totals
select
{[Date].[Calendar],[Date].[Calendar].[Calendar Year].members}
on columns
from
non visual
(select [Date].[Calendar].[Calendar Year].[CY 2002]:
[Date].[Calendar].[Calendar Year].[CY 2004] on columns
from [Adventure Works])
```

Result

All Periods	CY 2002	CY 2003	CY 2004
$80,450,596.98	$24,144,429.65	$32,202,669.43	$16,038,062.60

Analysis

The figure for All Periods is different. This happens to be the "real" total for All Periods. The previous query gave an "apparent" total. This time it's possible to work out the total for the two missing years by adding together CY 2002, CY 2003, and CY 2004 before subtracting that result from the All Periods value. Whether or not you have visual totals is a business decision.

Default Measure of a Cube

We'll soon be looking at subcubes. Subcubes are similar to subselects. One of the main differences you will find is that a subselect is part of one, and only one, query—it's query scoped. A subcube is session-scoped and can be used by multiple queries. Before we move on, it might be helpful to remind ourselves of the default measure of the cube.

Syntax

```
-- cube default measure
select [Measures].defaultmember
on columns
from
[Adventure Works]
```

Result

Reseller Sales Amount
$80,450,596.98

Analysis

The query contains the .defaultmember property function to verify that Reseller Sales Amount is the default measure. You might want to try .defaultmember against some of your non-measure dimension hierarchies.

Creating a Subcube

Subcubes are created differently from subselects. A subcube requires a Create statement. It does not return a cellset as it's created.

Syntax

```
-- a subcube
create subcube [Adventure Works] as
select
[Sales Reason].[Sales Reasons].[Reason Type].[Other]
on columns,
[Measures].[Internet Sales Amount]
on rows
from
[Adventure Works]
```

Result

```
Executing the query ...
Execution complete
```

Analysis

There are a few things to point out here. The Select does not actually execute because there is no cellset. The Select appears after the keyword As. The subcube must have the same name as the cube from which it's derived. Our subcube is called Adventure Works. The original Adventure Works cube has disappeared; fortunately, we can get it back! For the next query to work, don't close your query editor window.

Default Measure of a Subcube

[Adventure Works] in the From clause is the subcube, not the cube. It will only work as a subcube if you try this example in the same query window as the Create Subcube syntax.

Syntax

```
-- subcube default measure
select [Measures].defaultmember
on columns
from
[Adventure Works]
```

Result

Internet Sales Amount
$18,678,948.02

Analysis

The subcube contains only one measure, Internet Sales Amount. This is now our default measure. Be sure to keep your query editor window open for the next query.

Querying a Subcube

Querying a subcube is the same as querying a cube.

Syntax

```
-- querying a subcube
select
[Sales Reason].[Sales Reasons].[Reason Type]
on columns
from
[Adventure Works]
```

Result

Other
$18,678,948.02

Analysis

There is only one sales reason type (Other) because that was the only one specified in the Select during subcube creation.

Dropping a Subcube

To get back to the original cube, you have to drop the subcube.

Syntax

```
-- drop subcube
drop subcube [Adventure Works]
```

Result

```
Executing the query ...
Execution complete
```

Analysis

After this query has been run, your Select statements will work against the whole cube and no longer against the subcube. A less elegant approach involves closing and reopening the query editor window.

Subcube with Visual Totals

Now try the following three queries. Run them one at a time—the Create first (including the Select in parentheses), the standalone Select second, and, finally, the Drop.

Syntax

```
-- another subcube (visual totals)
create subcube [Adventure Works] as
(select [Date].[Calendar].[Calendar Year].[CY 2002]:
[Date].[Calendar].[Calendar Year].[CY 2004] on columns
from [Adventure Works])
-- query the subcube
select
{[Date].[Calendar],[Date].[Calendar].[Calendar Year].members}
on columns
from
[Adventure Works]
-- drop the subcube
drop subcube [Adventure Works]
```

Result

All Periods	CY 2002	CY 2003	CY 2004
$72,385,161.68	$24,144,429.65	$32,202,669.43	$16,038,062.60

Analysis

The three years add up to equal All Periods. Subcubes, by default (and like subselects), use visual totals. Only the result of the standalone Select is shown.

Subcube with Nonvisual Totals

Three separate steps again. Note the introduction of Non Visual immediately after the keyword As.

Syntax

```
-- another subcube (non visual totals)
create subcube [Adventure Works] as
non visual
(select [Date].[Calendar].[Calendar Year].[CY 2002]:
[Date].[Calendar].[Calendar Year].[CY 2004] on columns
from [Adventure Works])
-- query the subcube
select
{[Date].[Calendar],[Date].[Calendar].[Calendar Year].members}
on columns
from
[Adventure Works]
-- drop the subcube
drop subcube [Adventure Works]
```

Result

All Periods	CY 2002	CY 2003	CY 2004
$80,450,596.98	$24,144,429.65	$32,202,669.43	$16,038,062.60

Analysis

If you compare the All Periods cell with that of the last query, you can see the difference between subcubes with visual totals and those with nonvisual totals. The choice is yours.

Chapter 11

Not All There: Dealing with Empty Cells

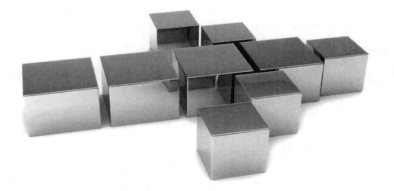

C ubes are often pretty big. They contain lots and lots of data. However, there will also be many gaps. For example, it's unlikely that every customer bought every product on every single day. There will be missing or null data. Sometimes, you want to see null values—maybe zero sales are of interest. Sometimes, the null values are a distraction and you will want to hide them. This chapter concentrates on displaying and hiding empty cells.

▶ **Key concepts**   Different ways of hiding empty cells

▶ **Keywords**   Non Empty, NonEmpty

Empty Cells

Often your queries will return empty cells. This may or may not be the result you desire. Sometimes, empty cells are simply a distraction and occupy too much real estate. Sometimes, empty cells reveal important information (for example, showing times when there were no sales).

Syntax

```
-- returns empty cells
select
{[Product].[Product Categories].[Category].[Accessories]}
on columns,
{[Date].[Calendar].[Calendar Year]} on rows
from
[Adventure Works]
where [Measures].[Internet Order Quantity]
```

Result

	Accessories
CY 2001	(null)
CY 2002	(null)
CY 2003	15,025
CY 2004	21,067
CY 2006	(null)

Analysis

The default behavior of MDX is to show empty cells. Here, the years CY 2001, CY 2002, and CY 2006 have empty cells for the Internet Order Quantity for Accessories. You might wish to hide these cells in your results. CY 2005 is missing altogether. This does not simply mean no sales for that year; it means the year itself is absent from the cube data.

Hiding Empty Cells

This time we have decided to suppress the empty cells using the Non Empty syntax. Whether you show or hide empty cells is a business decision.

Syntax

```
-- hides empty cells
select
{[Product].[Product Categories].[Category].[Accessories]}
on columns,
non empty {[Date].[Calendar].[Calendar Year]} on rows
from
[Adventure Works]
where [Measures].[Internet Order Quantity]
```

Result

	Accessories
CY 2003	15,025
CY 2004	21,067

Analysis

Note that Non Empty is two words; it's an MDX operator and does not require the use of parentheses. The effect is to hide the three years shown in the previous query that returned empty cells.

Another Way to Hide Cells

This time we have the NonEmpty function rather than the Non Empty operator. Try it, if you want, and notice the results are different from the previous query.

Syntax

```
-- hides one empty cell but not others
select
{[Product].[Product Categories].[Category].[Accessories]}
on columns,
```

```
nonempty({[Date].[Calendar].[Calendar Year]}) on rows
from
[Adventure Works]
where [Measures].[Internet Order Quantity]
```

Result

	Accessories
CY 2001	(null)
CY 2002	(null)
CY 2003	15,025
CY 2004	21,067

Analysis

Note that, this time, NonEmpty is one word and uses parentheses. NonEmpty is an MDX function. It often gives different results from the Non Empty operator. Maybe you were not expecting these results. CY 2006 is hidden, but CY 2001 and CY 2002 have returned even though there are two empty cells! This behavior is explored in the next couple queries.

More on NonEmpty

To try and establish whether the last query returned incorrect results, let's swap the Columns set with the measure in the Where clause.

Syntax

```
-- hides just the one empty cell
select
{[Measures].[Internet Order Quantity]}
on columns,
nonempty({[Date].[Calendar].[Calendar Year]}) on rows
from
[Adventure Works]
where [Product].[Product Categories].[Category].[Accessories]
```

Result

	Internet Order Quantity
CY 2001	(null)
CY 2002	(null)
CY 2003	15,025
CY 2004	21,067

Analysis

Not much luck! Why does one year get hidden and two years are shown with empty cells? When you first meet this behavior, it might seem quite strange. To resolve the paradox, take a look at the next few queries.

Explaining NonEmpty

This query adds another measure on the Columns axis. The NonEmpty function has been temporarily removed to help resolve its behavior.

Syntax

```
-- adding an extra measure
select
{[Measures].[Internet Order Quantity],[Measures].[Reseller Sales Amount]}
on columns,
{[Date].[Calendar].[Calendar Year]} on rows
from
[Adventure Works]
where [Product].[Product Categories].[Category].[Accessories]
```

Result

	Internet Order Quantity	Reseller Sales Amount
CY 2001	(null)	$20,235.36
CY 2002	(null)	$92,735.35
CY 2003	15,025	$296,532.88
CY 2004	21,067	$161,794.33
CY 2006	(null)	(null)

Analysis

There are three empty cells for Internet Order Quantity and one empty cell for Reseller Sales Amount. Both of the measures have empty cells for CY 2006.

NonEmpty with a Different Measure

Here we are using the new measure by itself to see what happens when NonEmpty is reintroduced. The query is identical (apart from the measure chosen) to the one that used Internet Order Quantity earlier.

Syntax

```
-- the extra measure alone seems to work
select
{[Measures].[Reseller Sales Amount]}
on columns,
nonempty({[Date].[Calendar].[Calendar Year]}) on rows
from
[Adventure Works]
where [Product].[Product Categories].[Category].[Accessories]
```

Result

	Reseller Sales Amount
CY 2001	$20,235.36
CY 2002	$92,735.35
CY 2003	$296,532.88
CY 2004	$161,794.33

Analysis

This time, it works as expected. The single empty cell for CY 2006 for Reseller Sales Amount is suppressed. Confusing? Why does it appear to work for one measure yet not for another measure? The next query might help.

This Time NonEmpty Produces Different Results

The NonEmpty function (unlike the Non Empty operator) accepts an extra parameter. Here the parameter is Internet Order Quantity for the first query, and for the second query it's Reseller Sales Amount.

Syntax

```
-- nonempty with a measure specified for the empty test
select
{[Measures].[Internet Order Quantity] ,[Measures].[Reseller Sales Amount]}
on columns,
nonempty({[Date].[Calendar].[Calendar Year]},[Measures]
.[Internet Order Quantity]) on rows
from
[Adventure Works]
where [Product].[Product Categories].[Category].[Accessories]
-- nonempty with a different measure specified for the empty test
select
{[Measures].[Internet Order Quantity] ,[Measures].[Reseller Sales Amount]}
on columns,
```

```
nonempty({ [Date].[Calendar].[Calendar Year]},
[Measures].[Reseller Sales Amount]) on rows
from
[Adventure Works]
where [Product].[Product Categories].[Category].[Accessories]
```

Result

	Internet Order Quantity	Reseller Sales Amount
CY 2003	15,025	$296,532.88
CY 2004	21,067	$161,794.33

	Internet Order Quantity	Reseller Sales Amount
CY 2001	(null)	$20,235.36
CY 2002	(null)	$92,735.35
CY 2003	15,025	$296,532.88
CY 2004	21,067	$161,794.33

Analysis

At last! If you examine the result from the first query, it finally displays the answer we were expecting earlier. The empty cells for CY 2001, CY 2002, and CY 2006 for Internet Order Quantity are hidden. If you were to remove the Reseller Sales Amount from the Columns axis, you would arrive at the same results for Internet Order Quantity. The second parameter for NonEmpty is the measure to test for emptiness—it's looking for empty cells for Internet Order Quantity.

The second query tests Reseller Sales Amount for emptiness. When you look at the Internet Order Quantity column, you will notice that the output is the same as when we first used the NonEmpty function a few queries ago. To verify this, try removing Reseller Sales Amount from the Columns axis.

Finally, here's an explanation. The Non Empty operator removes empty cells for whichever measure you incorporate into the query. The NonEmpty function removes empty cells for whichever measure you include as a second parameter to the function. If you omit the second parameter, the function will test the default measure (unless another measure is specified in the Where clause) for the cube for emptiness. The default measure for this cube happens to be Reseller Sales Amount. You can test this by writing a [Measures].DefaultMember query, as shown here:

```
Select
[Measures].defaultmember on columns
from
[Adventure Works]
```

Reseller Sales Amount
$80,450,596.98

Chapter 12

Smiley Faces: Working with Key Performance Indicators (KPIs)

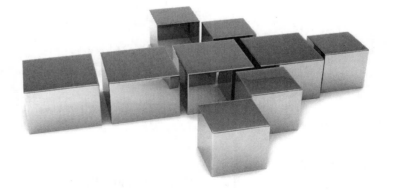

K ey performance indicators (KPIs) are a vital part of business intelligence. At a glance, you can see how well you are doing without having to dig down and analyze individual metrics. They provide a high-level overview of results—and of results against targets. In this chapter we explore using, modifying, formatting, and creating KPIs in MDX.

▶ **Key concepts**   KPI value, goal, status, and trend

▶ **Keywords**   Select, KPIValue, KPIGoal, KPIStatus, KPITrend, format_string, With Member, .currentmember, Create KPI, VBA!Format

Selecting KPIs

If you have KPIs (key performance indicators) as part of your cube design back in BIDS, you can select them in an MDX query. If you don't have existing KPIs, you can create them as part of your query. You will see how to do this shortly.

Syntax

```
-- selecting existing KPIs
select
crossjoin([Date].[Fiscal].[Fiscal Year].[FY 2003],
{KPIValue("Product Gross Profit Margin"),
KPIGoal("Product Gross Profit Margin"),
KPIStatus("Product Gross Profit Margin")})
on columns,
[Product].[Product Categories].[Category]
on rows
from [Adventure Works]
```

Result

	FY 2003	FY 2003	FY 2003
	Gross Profit Margin	Product Gross Profit Margin Goal	Product Gross Profit Margin Status
Accessories	29.23%	0.4	-1
Bikes	9.80%	0.12	0
Clothing	23.46%	0.2	1
Components	12.40%	0.1	1

Analysis

The query uses KPIValue, KPIGoal, and KPIStatus. There is also KPITrend, which is not used in this query. The results show the KPI by Category for FY 2003. The KPIStatus indicates how close the KPIValue is to the KPIGoal. Note the column header for KPIValue reflects the original measure used in the KPI design in BIDS and looks slightly different from the KPIGoal and KPIStatus headers. Also, the KPIValue and the KPIGoal are not in the same format.

Formatting KPIs

Here the KPIs are redone as measures. This fixes a number of problems in the previous query. The KPITrend has been added and two years are shown to illustrate how KPITrend works.

Syntax

```
-- formatting existing KPIs
with member [Measures].[Actual] as
KPIValue("Product Gross Profit Margin"),format_string = "Percent"
member [Measures].[Target] as
KPIGoal("Product Gross Profit Margin"),format_string="Percent"
member [Measures].[Status] as KPIStatus("Product Gross Profit Margin")
member [Measures].[Trend] as KPITrend("Product Gross Profit Margin")
select
crossjoin({[Date].[Fiscal].[Fiscal Year].[FY 2003],
[Date].[Fiscal].[Fiscal Year].[FY 2004]},{[Measures].[Actual],
[Measures].[Target],[Measures].[Status],[Measures].[Trend]})
on columns,
[Product].[Product Categories].[Category]
on rows
from [Adventure Works]
```

Result

	FY 2003	FY 2003	FY 2003	FY 2003	FY 2004	FY 2004	FY 2004	FY 2004
	Actual	Target	Status	Trend	Actual	Target	Status	Trend
Accessories	29.23%	40.00%	-1	-1	52.19%	40.00%	1	1
Bikes	9.80%	12.00%	0	-1	11.35%	12.00%	1	1
Clothing	23.46%	20.00%	1	-1	14.74%	20.00%	-1	-1
Components	12.40%	10.00%	1	1	5.91%	10.00%	-1	-1

Analysis

The KPITrend (renamed as Trend) for this particular KPI shows the change in the KPIValue from year to year. The column headers for the KPI are now more readable and the KPIGoal (renamed as Target) is formatted the same as KPIValue (renamed as Actual) to make the KPIStatus (renamed as Status) figure easier to understand.

Changing KPIs

Sometimes you may want to temporarily override the original KPI definition created back in BIDS. In this query, both the KPIGoal and the KPIStatus for the Accessories category have been overridden.

Syntax

```
-- changing existing KPIGoal (target) and KPIStatus
with member [Measures].[Actual] as
KPIValue("Product Gross Profit Margin"),format_string = "Percent"
member [Measures].[Target] as
iif([Product].[Product Categories].currentmember is
[Product].[Product Categories].[Accessories],.60,
KPIGoal("Product Gross Profit Margin")),format_string="Percent"
member [Measures].[Status] as
iif([Product].[Product Categories].currentmember is
[Product].[Product Categories].[Accessories],
Case
When  [Measures].[Actual]/ [Measures].[Target]
>= .95
Then 1
When  [Measures].[Actual]/ [Measures].[Target]
<  .95
And
[Measures].[Actual]/ [Measures].[Target]
>= .70
Then 0
Else -1
End
,KPIStatus("Product Gross Profit Margin"))
select
crossjoin({[Date].[Fiscal].[Fiscal Year].[FY 2003],
[Date].[Fiscal].[Fiscal Year].[FY 2004]},
{[Measures].[Actual],[Measures].[Target],[Measures].[Status]})
on columns,
[Product].[Product Categories].[Category]
on rows
from [Adventure Works]
```

Result

	FY 2003	FY 2003	FY 2003	FY 2004	FY 2004	FY 2004
	Actual	Target	Status	Actual	Target	Status
Accessories	29.23%	60.00%	-1	52.19%	60.00%	0
Bikes	9.80%	12.00%	0	11.35%	12.00%	1
Clothing	23.46%	20.00%	1	14.74%	20.00%	-1
Components	12.40%	10.00%	1	5.91%	10.00%	-1

Analysis

The KPIGoal (target) has been set to 60% instead of the original 40%—a little more demanding! The KPIStatus (status) is also a more challenging figure. It has been changed, for the lifetime of the query only, to qualify as a status of 1 only when the KPIValue is more than 95% of the KPIGoal—the original threshold was 90%. Thus, the KPIValue (actual) for Accessories for FY 2004 results in a status of 0, even though profits were pretty good at 52.19%.

Creating KPIs

SSAS 2008 introduces the new Create KPI syntax. Unfortunately, if you are using SSAS 2005, this is not available. The workaround in SSAS 2005 is to create your own measures. If you do have SSAS 2008, run the two Creates together (the Go statement allows you to do this without a syntax error) before you try the Select.

Syntax

```
-- creating a new KPI
create member [Adventure Works].[Measures].[Profit Margin Value] as
[Measures].[Gross Profit Margin]
go
create KPI [Adventure Works].[Profit Margin] as
[Measures].[Profit Margin Value],
goal=
case
when [Product].[Category].CurrentMember Is [Product].[Category]
.[Accessories]
then vba!format(.40,"Percent")
when [Product].[Category].CurrentMember Is [Product].[Category].[Bikes]
then vba!format(.12,"Percent")
when [Product].[Category].CurrentMember Is [Product].[Category].[Clothing]
then vba!format(.20,"Percent")
when [Product].[Category].CurrentMember Is [Product].[Category]
```

```
. [Components]
then vba!format(.10,"Percent")
else vba!format(.12,"Percent")
end,
status=
case
when
vba!cDBL(left(KPIValue("Profit Margin"),len(KPIValue("Profit Margin"))-1))
* 100/vba!cDBL(left(KPIGoal("Profit Margin"),
len(KPIGoal("Profit Margin"))-1)) >= .90
then 1
when
vba!cDBL(left(KPIValue("Profit Margin"),
len(KPIValue("Profit Margin"))-1))
* 100/vba!cDBL(left(KPIGoal("Profit Margin"),
len(KPIGoal("Profit Margin"))-1)) <  .90
and
vba!cDBL(left(KPIValue("Profit Margin"),
len(KPIValue("Profit Margin"))-1)) * 100/
vba!cDBL(left(KPIGoal("Profit Margin"),
len(KPIGoal("Profit Margin"))-1)) >= .80
then 0
else -1
end
-- selecting the new KPI
select
crossjoin({[Date].[Fiscal].[Fiscal Year].[FY 2003],
[Date].[Fiscal].[Fiscal Year].[FY 2004]},
{KPIValue("Profit Margin"),KPIGoal("Profit Margin"),
KPIStatus("Profit Margin")})
on columns,
[Product].[Product Categories].[Category]
on rows
from [Adventure Works]
```

Result

	FY 2003	FY 2003	FY 2003	FY 2004	FY 2004	FY 2004
	Profit Margin Value	Profit Margin Goal	Profit Margin Status	Profit Margin Value	Profit Margin Goal	Profit Margin Status
Accessories	29.23%	40.00%	-1	52.19%	40.00%	1
Bikes	9.80%	12.00%	0	11.35%	12.00%	1
Clothing	23.46%	20.00%	1	14.74%	20.00%	-1
Components	12.40%	10.00%	1	5.91%	10.00%	-1

Analysis

The Select is reasonably straightforward. The Create Member is there so the KPI column headers have consistent names. The Create KPI is rather more complex. Note the Goal= and Status= entries; there is no corresponding Value= as you might expect. VBA Format is used to show KPIValue and KPIGoal as percentages. In addition, there is heavy use of other VBA functions to enable comparison of KPIValue and KPIGoal in the Status= section for defining KPIStatus. It is necessary to remove the % symbol introduced in the previous formatting. The KPIStatus for Bikes for FY 2004 is 1 because the KPIValue is more than 90% of the KPIGoal. You can also include a Trend= section, if you wish, in the Create KPI syntax.

There is often more than one way to accomplish the same result in MDX. The following syntax shows an alternative you may find easier to read (it eliminates the VBA functions):

```
create member [Adventure Works].[Measures].[Profit Margin Value] as
[Measures].[Gross Profit Margin]
go
create member [Adventure Works].[Measures].[Profit Margin Goal] as
case
when [Product].[Category].CurrentMember Is [Product].[Category]
.[Accessories]
then 0.40
when [Product].[Category].CurrentMember Is [Product].[Category].[Bikes]
then 0.12
when [Product].[Category].CurrentMember Is [Product].[Category].[Clothing]
then 0.20
when [Product].[Category].CurrentMember Is [Product].[Category]
.[Components]
then 0.10
else 0.12
end,
FORMAT_STRING = "Percent"
go
create member [Adventure Works].[Measures].[Profit Margin Status] as
case
when
KPIValue("Profit Margin")/KPIGoal("Profit Margin") >= .90
then 1
when
KPIValue("Profit Margin")/KPIGoal("Profit Margin") <  .90
and
KPIValue("Profit Margin")/KPIGoal("Profit Margin") >= .80
```

```
then 0
else -1
end
go
create KPI [Adventure Works].[Profit Margin] as
[Measures].[Profit Margin Value],
goal=
[Measures].[Profit Margin Goal],
status=
[Measures].[Profit Margin Status]
```

Undoing Create

Both Create Member and Create KPI result in session-level objects that can be reused later in the same query editor window. It's a good idea to clean up session-level objects when you are finished with them.

Syntax

```
-- cleaning up
drop KPI [Adventure Works].[Profit Margin]
go
drop member [Adventure Works].[Measures].[Profit Margin Value]
```

Result

```
Executing the query ... 01.
Execution complete 01.

Executing the query ... 11.
Execution complete 11.
```

Analysis

The Go statement allows both Drop commands to be run together without a syntax error.

Chapter 13

Hodgepodge: A Chapter of Miscellaneous Techniques

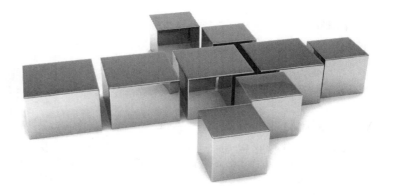

This is a catchall chapter for topics that do not fit easily into earlier chapters. Formatting and conditional formatting are investigated. There are also queries to drill through and drill down on the cube.

▶   **Key concepts**   Formatting, conditional formatting, dimension member aliases, measures member aliases, drill through, drill down

▶   **Keywords**   VBA!Format, Case, With Member, Drillthrough, DrillDownMember

Conditional Formatting Base Query

You've met the Format_String setting for measures many times now. That's an MDX construct. But you can extend MDX by embedding VBA (Visual Basic for Applications) and Excel syntax. This facility is going to be exploited to give an example of conditional formatting on a measure in the next query. Here's a base query to get us started.

Syntax

```
-- conditional formatting base query
select
[Measures].[Internet Sales Amount]
on columns,
{[Customer].[Customer Geography].[Country].[France],
[Customer].[Customer Geography].[Country].[United Kingdom],
[Customer].[Customer Geography].[Country].[United States]}
on rows
from
[Adventure Works]
```

Result

	Internet Sales Amount
France	$2,644,017.71
United Kingdom	$3,391,712.21
United States	$9,389,789.51

Analysis

This result may or may not be what you want. If all of your sales are recorded in U.S. dollars, it's fine. But possibly, your sales were recorded in local currencies. That's a situation where you might find conditional formatting helpful.

Conditional Formatting

To use VBA syntax inside MDX, you use VBA! followed by the name of the function. Here we are looking at VBA Format. For Excel functions you would type Excel! first.

Syntax

```
-- conditional formatting
with member [Measures].[Sales in Local Currency] as
case
when [Customer].[Customer Geography].currentmember.name = "France"
then vba!format([Measures].[Internet Sales Amount],"#,###.00€")
when [Customer].[Customer Geography].currentmember.name = "United Kingdom"
then vba!format([Measures].[Internet Sales Amount],"£#,###.00")
when [Customer].[Customer Geography].currentmember.name = "United States"
then vba!format([Measures].[Internet Sales Amount],"$#,###.00")
end
select
[Measures].[Sales in Local Currency]
on columns,
{[Customer].[Customer Geography].[Country].[France],
[Customer].[Customer Geography].[Country].[United Kingdom],
[Customer].[Customer Geography].[Country].[United States]}
on rows
from
[Adventure Works]
```

Result

	Sales in Local Currency
France	2,644,017.71€
United Kingdom	£3,391,712.21
United States	$9,389,789.51

Analysis

The .name property of the .currentmember property function simply gives us the name of the country. The Case construct applies the appropriate VBA!Format to the sales amount.

With large dimensions, the preceding syntax may not be the most efficient from a performance point of view. You may like to also try the following alternative syntax (notice it uses the Is operator and the key value of a member):

```
with member [Measures].[Sales in Local Currency] as
case
when [Customer].[Customer Geography].currentmember is
[Customer].[Customer Geography].[Country].&[France]
then vba!format([Measures].[Internet Sales Amount],"#,###.00€")
when [Customer].[Customer Geography].currentmember is
[Customer].[Customer Geography].[Country].&[United Kingdom]
then vba!format([Measures].[Internet Sales Amount],"£#,###.00")
when [Customer].[Customer Geography].currentmember is
[Customer].[Customer Geography].[Country].&[United States]
then vba!format([Measures].[Internet Sales Amount],"$#,###.00")
end
select
[Measures].[Sales in Local Currency]
on columns,
{[Customer].[Customer Geography].[Country].[France],
[Customer].[Customer Geography].[Country].[United Kingdom],
[Customer].[Customer Geography].[Country].[United States]}
on rows
from
[Adventure Works]
```

Measure Member Aliases

This is a simple calculated measure. It's not really much of a calculation but just shows how to alias a measure.

Syntax

```
-- aliases for measures members
with member [Measures].[Customer Sales] as
[Measures].[Internet Sales Amount]
select
[Measures].[Customer Sales]
on columns
from
[Adventure Works]
```

Result

Analysis

Hopefully, by this stage of the book, this query is a revision for you!

Non-measure Dimension Member Aliases

You can also alias members of non-measure dimensions if you wish.

Syntax

```
-- aliases for dimension members
with member [Product].[Product Categories].[Cycles]
as [Product].[Product Categories].[Category].[Bikes]
select
[Product].[Product Categories].[Cycles]
on columns
from
[Adventure Works]
```

Result

Analysis

We have changed Bikes to Cycles. This is a calculated member; it is not a calculated measure. The syntax is [Dimension].[Hierarchy].[name].

DrillDownMember

DrillDownMember is an often-overlooked but very handy function.

Syntax

```
-- drilldownmember
with member [Measures].[Level in Hierarchy]
as [Customer].[Customer Geography].currentmember.level.ordinal
select
```

```
{ [Measures].[Customer Count],[Measures].[Level in Hierarchy]}
on columns,
nonempty
(drilldownmember(
{[Customer].[Customer Geography].[Country].[United States]},
{[Customer].[Customer Geography].[Country].[United States],
[Customer].[Customer Geography].[State-Province].[California]},recursive),
[Measures].[Customer Count])
on rows
from
[Adventure Works]
```

Result

	Customer Count	Level in Hierarchy
United States	7,819	1
Alabama	1	2
Arizona	2	2
California	4,444	2
Barstow	1	3
Bell Gardens	1	3
Bellflower	194	3
Berkeley	200	3
Beverly Hills	188	3
Burbank	192	3

Analysis

Not the easiest syntax in the book! This one requires a little bit of practice. It might be worth it. It allows us to see the children of California right next to California and not further down the rows. In order to help you decipher the result, I've also shown the level of each row entry with .currentmember.level.ordinal.

DrillDownMember accepts either two or three parameters. In the example, it compares the members of the first and second sets (the first and second parameters) and drills down on members that are common to both sets—here it's United States. If the third Recursive parameter (which is optional) is included, it compares the result set from the first two parameters once more against the second set and drills down on members that are common to both—here it's California.

Drillthrough 1/2

When you look at the values of cells in a cellset, they may be aggregated. Drillthrough (as opposed to drilldown) lets you break the aggregation apart into the individual "records" that comprise the aggregation. This is a base query for the next query.

Syntax

```
-- drillthrough 1/2
-- 4099.09
select
[Measures].[Internet Sales Amount] on columns
from
[Adventure Works]
where ([Product].[Product Categories].[Category].[Bikes],
[Customer].[Customer Geography].[Country].[United States],
[Date].[Calendar].[Date].[July 1, 2001])
```

Result

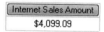

Internet Sales Amount
$4,099.09

Analysis

Internet sales of bikes in the United States on July 1, 2001, were $4,099.09—but for which bike(s) and for which customer(s)?

Drillthrough 2/2

Let's try a drillthrough query.

Syntax

```
-- drillthrough 2/2
-- 3399.99 and 699.0982
drillthrough maxrows 100
select
[Measures].[Internet Sales Amount] on columns
from
[Adventure Works]
where ([Product].[Product Categories].[Category].[Bikes],
[Customer].[Customer Geography].[Country].[United States],
[Date].[Calendar].[Date].[July 1, 2001])
return
[$Product].[Product],Key([$Product].[Product]),
[$Date].[Date],[$Measures].[Internet Sales Amount],[$Customer].[Customer],
[$Customer].[State-Province],[$Customer].[City]
```

Result

[$Product].[Product]	[$Product].[Product]	[$Date].[Date]	[Internet Sales].[Internet Sales Amount]	[$Customer].[Customer]	[$Customer].[State-Province]	[$Customer].[City]
Mountain-100 Silver, 44	346	July 1, 2001	3399.99	Sydney S. Wright	Oregon	Lebanon
Road-650 Black, 62	336	July 1, 2001	699.0982	Ruben Prasad	California	Beverly Hills

Analysis

A single aggregation has been decomposed into two "records." The value of the sales are 3399.99 and 699.0982, which give us the total in the previous query (aside from a bit of rounding). So, two customers (from Oregon and California) bought a bike each on July 1, 2001. The $ prefix is used to refer to a dimension (including the Measures dimension). The Key function is used to return the key value of a member. Additional functions include Name and MemberValue, which you may like to try (in our example they make little difference to the result).

Chapter 14

After You Finish

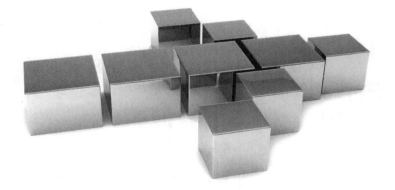

Where to Use MDX

Throughout this book, you've been using SSMS to write your MDX queries and display the results. It's unlikely that your users will have SSMS—indeed, it's not recommended for end users because it's simply too powerful and potentially dangerous. This chapter presents some alternative software and methods for getting MDX query results to the end user.

SSRS

SSRS can generate simple MDX for you, but you may want some of the more sophisticated queries you've seen in this book. You will need an SSAS connection to do this. To use your own MDX, click the Design Mode button on the toolbar while in Query Designer in SSRS. You are then able to paste in the code you might have developed in SSMS. Here's an example:

```
Select [Date].[Calendar].[Calendar Year] on columns,
[Product].[Product Categories].[Category] on rows
from
[Adventure Works]
where [Measures].[Reseller Sales Amount]
```

Unfortunately, SSRS will generate an error. It only likes measures on columns. So you have to put the measure on the columns and crossjoin the other dimensions on the rows. Here's the same code adapted to work with SSRS:

```
Select [Measures].[Reseller Sales Amount] on columns,
crossjoin([Date].[Calendar].[Calendar Year],
[Product].[Product Categories].[Category])
on rows
from
[Adventure Works]
```

If you then opt for a matrix design, you can easily drag the calendar years back onto the columns.

SSIS

With SSIS you can get the MDX results into a data pipeline using a Data Flow task. It's then quite easy to convert this into a text file, an Excel worksheet, or an SQL Server table. You will need an OLE DB or ADO.NET source with an SSAS connection. Next, you need to change the data access mode from Table or View to SQL command and then paste in your MDX from SSMS.

SQL

You can embed MDX inside an SQL query. This allows you to exploit any SQL Server frontends you may already have. One way to accomplish this is to set up a linked server to SSAS from SQL Server and paste the MDX into an Openquery construct.

DMX

If you need to train an SSAS data-mining model or run a DMX prediction query against a cube, you can use MDX inside the DMX.

XMLA

Your MDX queries can also be nested inside XMLA. To do so, use an <Execute> <Command> <Statement> construct.

Winforms and Webforms

If you are a .NET developer, you can create your own Windows applications (Winforms) or Web pages (Webforms) to display the results of your MDX queries. The simplest way to do so is to use a datagrid. Your application will need a reference to Microsoft. AnalysisServices.AdomdClient. The MDX can return the data as a dataset, a datareader, a cellset, or as XML. Here's some sample VB.NET code that creates a dataset (you may have to adapt the Data Source and Initial Catalog properties as well as the cube name in the From clause):

```
Imports Microsoft.AnalysisServices.AdomdClient

Dim con As New AdomdConnection("Data Source=localhost;
Initial Catalog=Adventure Works DW")
con.open()
Dim cmd As New AdomdCommand
("select [Date].[Calendar].[Calendar Year] on columns, [Product]
.[Product Categories].[Category] on rows from [Adventure Works]
where [Measures].[Reseller Sales Amount]", con)
Dim adt As New AdomdDataAdapter(cmd)
Dim dst As New DataSet
adt.Fill(dst)

    'or use a DATAREADER
    'Dim rdr As AdomdDataReader = cmd.ExecuteReader
    'do stuff with reader
    'rdr.Close()
```

```
'or use a CELLSET
'Dim cst As CellSet = cmd.ExecuteCellSet
'do stuff with cellset

'or use an XMLREADER
'Dim xml As System.Xml.XmlReader = cmd.ExecuteXmlReader
'do stuff with XML
```

```
DataGridView1.DataSource = dst.Tables(0)
'for a Webform add .DataBind
con.Close()
```

Performance Point Server and ProClarity

Both Microsoft Office Performance Point Server and ProClarity allow you to directly paste in MDX.

Third-Party Software

An infinite variety of third-party software applications are available that allow you to paste in your MDX.

Copy and Paste

You can right-click the Results pane in SSMS, choose Select All, right-click again, and then choose Copy. You can then paste the MDX results (rather than the MDX itself) into an application of your choice.

Index